To be Confirmed...

To be Confirmed...

by

GAVIN REID

HODDER AND STOUGHTON
LONDON SYDNEY AUCKLAND TORONTO

Biblical Quotations are from the Good News Bible (Today's English Version) published by the Bible Society and Collins, and used with permission.

Contents

FOR MARTIN PARSONS
who prepared me for confirmation
and got across to me something of
the thrill of Christian beliefs.

And for EMILY PARSONS
who smiled away in the background
and simply lived it out.

About this book

I have tried to write a book that is easy and enjoyable to read and yet at the same time tries to teach some basic truths. What I have in mind is that this book would be read at the rate of a chapter a week, and that a group of confirmation candidates could meet each week to discuss and think further on the ground each chapter covers. There are discussion questions with each chapter.

So – after the introductory chapter, that means we have a twelve-week course.

I have tried to write this for young people in their mid- and late teenage years – but if others find it suitable, so much the better.

Young people are amongst the deepest and most searching thinkers and questioners and I am well aware that so much more could have been said. Let me assure any reader who finds any chapter to be saying too little or to be unconvincing, that there are plenty of other, good books around – to say nothing of wise Christian heads.

I would like to thank Stephen my eldest son for proving that this book can be read by a fifteen-year-old whose mind is full of motor-bikes, and especially my good friend Kay Pither for typing and retyping it so faithfully.

Gavin Reid

1: To be Confirmed . . .

Those who know me find it hard to believe – but I was once an officer in the Royal Air Force!

To get to such a 'lofty' position I had to go to what was known as an *Officer Cadet Training Unit*. After three months' fairly demanding training and the sitting of some examinations I was told I had passed the course and would be commissioned as an officer.

Changing from the life of a cadet to the life of an officer was marked by a *passing-out parade*. The name was well chosen for on at least one such occasion someone I know really did pass out! He was a tough sporting youngster who played tennis at Wimbledon. But after standing at attention for several moments – down he went; poor man!

DON'T PASS OUT – PASS IN!

The Confirmation service in the Church of England is not so much a passing-out parade, as a *passing-in parade!* It marks the day when you and I make official the fact that we want to be Christians and members of God's 'forces' here on earth – members of a church.

Let me be quite frank about this. The Confirmation Register books of many churches are often pretty sad reading. Many a name in the pages is that of someone who has hardly been seen since Confirmation Day. Somehow many people seem to look upon it as a passing-out from the Church rather than a *passing-in*.

LIKE A WEDDING

In a sense Confirmation is rather like a wedding. The important thing is what lies ahead, not what lies behind. A wedding marks the moment of two people *passing into* life together. In just the same way, Confirmation marks the moment when we pass into life together with God as our Father, and the other church members as our brothers and sisters.

If that is not what you want – then you must not go forward for Confirmation.

Sometimes older people, for the very best reasons, urge us to get confirmed because 'it's about time you were.' But the only time when you should get confirmed is when you are ready.

WHEN AM I READY FOR CONFIRMATION?

You are ready for Confirmation when:
1. You have learned enough about God.
2. You have learned enough about yourself.

... ABOUT GOD

Let's look at both these points. *First we need to know enough about God.* Here again it's very much like getting married. It would be madness not to know something about the boy or girl with whom you are going to share the rest of your life! To want to know what he or she is like, is common sense.

In the same way, if we are going to share the rest of our lives with God as our heavenly Father and with his son, Jesus Christ, as our ruler and guide; then we must find out whether he exists and what he is like. As you read these words you may not be sure. Don't worry – that's fine for the time being. This book is meant to help you find out more about God and his ways.

And I hope that as well as reading this book, bit by bit over the weeks, you will also be a member of a Confirmation group which is thinking together about what God is like. The great thing to remember is that if you really want to learn about God – you will. *He* will make sure of that!

... ABOUT OURSELVES

Secondly – *we need to know enough about ourselves*. It's very important on Confirmation Day to be sure you know what you are doing. Are you sure you are ready to make such a big decision – because that's what it is? You are going to be put on the spot and asked, in public by the bishop, some very important questions.

In what is known as the 'Series Two' Confirmation service there are three questions that the bishop will ask you which are all about *what you are doing*. Let's look at them.

Bishop: Do you turn to Christ?
You: *I turn to Christ.*

Bishop: Do you repent of your sins?
You: *I repent of my sins.*

Bishop: Do you renounce evil?
You: *I renounce evil.*

Now these are big things to say. You are saying before God, your parents and friends and many others that you have definitely decided to turn away from a life which is wrong in God's eyes. You now want Jesus Christ to be the leader of your life from day to day; and as you follow him you will have nothing to do with anything that is evil and wrong.

If you are to answer those questions honestly, you must

11

know what sort of a person you really want to be. Are you sure you know?

HOWEVER ...

It may well be that all this is a bit off-putting. You've hardly opened this book and here I am hammering at you with uncomfortable questions!

Let me suggest that you don't worry for the moment. The truth is that you may not be clear as to how much you know about God or yourself. The whole point of a Confirmation book and a Confirmation course is to help you sort these things out. By the time you've got to the end, the chances are that you *will* know one way or the other.

The big thing *then* is to be honest. If you really want to go forward, do so. If you are still not sure, then wait until the next time there is a Confirmation service, and keep on thinking.

BUT WHAT IS A CONFIRMATION SERVICE ALL ABOUT?

We have seen that the Confirmation service marks an occasion in your life – a big occasion. At your Confirmation service:

1. *You say publicly that you want to be a member of the Church – God's forever family.*
2. *The Church says publicly that you have become a member of the family, because you have been born all over again by God's Holy Spirit.*

1. ACTION REPLAY

Now there is a sense in which your Confirmation is an action replay of what took place when you were baptised. In the Church of England and some (but not all) other Christian churches, the children of those who say they are Christians are baptised as babies. They are promised to God

12

by their parents and godparents. The same sort of questions that you are asked at your Confirmation were put to your godparents when you were baptised (or 'Christened' as it is often called). They answered those questions on your behalf.

But of course you were too young to have learned anything about God and learned anything about yourself.

On Confirmation Day everybody takes for granted that you now know what you believe about God, and you are old enough and sensible enough to know your own mind.

So it's over to you! This is the action replay of your baptism, only this time no one makes your promises for you.

2. GOD IS CALLED IN

But being a Christian, I'm glad to say, is far more than a matter of us trying our hardest to keep our promises to God. *Being a Christian is proving that God keeps his promises to us!* Centuries ago the Apostle Peter was surrounded by a large crowd of people who wanted to become Christians. They asked him what they had to do – and this is his reply:

> Each one of you must turn away from his sins and be baptised in the name of Jesus Christ, so that your sins will be forgiven; and you will receive God's gift, the Holy Spirit.[1]

If you read these words carefully you will see three things:

a) They talk about what we have to do, and what the Confirmation promises are about: *'Turn away from your sins . . .'*

b) They talk about Baptism and the message that the Baptism ceremony contains – which is *that our sins are forgiven by God.*

1. Acts 2:38

13

c) They talk about God's gift to us when we turn to him –
which is that *he himself comes into our lives by the Holy
Spirit*.

Now it is this third point that lies at the centre of the
Confirmation service. We are not only confirming our
promises to God, *he* is confirming his promise to us. The
Christian is someone who is filled with God's Holy Spirit.

So on Confirmation Day one of the senior ministers in the
Church, a bishop, comes specially to take charge of the
service, and his big prayer for those who have come to be
confirmed is all about the Holy Spirit. This is what he says:

Send forth upon them thy Holy Spirit;
the Spirit of wisdom and understanding;
the Spirit of counsel and inward strength;
the Spirit of knowledge and true godliness;
and fill them, O Lord, with the Spirit of thy holy fear.

What a fantastic Spirit he is talking about! And as
the bishop lays his hands on the head of each person who
has come to be confirmed, it brings home to them in a
wonderful way, the sense of God's own fatherly hand giving
us strength and help to live for him.

There is no magic in the bishop's hand, of course! If we
do not really want to put our trust fully in God then all the
hands of all the bishops in the world couldn't give us the
Holy Spirit. But if we really mean business with God, then
the touch of that senior Christian's hand will be a wonderful
reminder to us that God's gift of the Holy Spirit is well and
truly ours.

Again Almighty God doesn't have to wait until a bishop
touches us before he can send his Spirit into our lives. For
many of us our Confirmation Day only *confirms* what has
already happened.

The great thing is that God comes to us by his Spirit as

we come to him in our trusting, and that is why we can be born again into his family the Church. And Confirmation Day puts over *that* message loud and clear.

3. WE ARE SENT OUT

The Confirmation service is our *passing-in parade* as far as joining the Church is concerned. But it also is, after all, a sort of *passing-out parade*, in spite of all I said earlier on.

When you join God's Church, you are joining a group of people who have got a job to do. And that job is to go and live for God our Father and to serve him in daily life. This may sound rather hard work, and oh so serious!

But the experience of countless thousands of Christians over the years is that it is the most worthwhile way of living any man or woman can find.

Questions
1. When is someone ready to be confirmed?
2. How much is being a Christian to do with someone keeping promises to God?
3. What are the promises God wants to keep with us?
4. Do I need to have been through a Confirmation service before I can be called a Christian?

Passages to Read
(recommended version – *Good News Bible*)
1. Acts 2:37–42
2. Col. 1:9–14 (St. Paul's prayer for new Christians.)

2: The Man who was Different

'As far as I'm concerned,' said Harry (who was always nicknamed 'Professor' on account of his low-slung spectacles!), 'Jesus was a great teacher. One of the best. We can all learn from him.'

'That's right!' said Jill, combing her hair yet again. 'A great teacher, but Arthur's stuff about Son of God doesn't make sense. I bet Jesus never said he was. It was just those Apostle blokes!'

'But Jesus did pretty well say he was God,' argued John, who was beginning to feel exasperated. 'The trouble with you lot is you make sweeping statements about Jesus but you never bother to read the Bible for yourselves!'

'Temper, temper,' chided Jill. And John, for all his resolutions about loving people, could have socked her one...

* * *

I've been involved in plenty of conversations like this one and I expect you've been over that ground too. Perhaps you find yourself siding with Jill and 'the Professor' rather than with John.

Fair enough. But first of all just stop to realise what an amazing thing is happening. Centuries after Jesus of Nazareth was executed by the Romans with full approval by most of the crowds who were in Jerusalem at the time – we are still arguing about him!

This book is about *Christ*ianity. I say this reverently – it is not about *God*-ianity but Christianity. And the reason is simple. We Christians believe that Jesus is the key person who unlocks the secret of what God is really like. So let's see how and what we know about Jesus.

HOW DO WE KNOW ABOUT JESUS?

In the middle of the first century A.D. several men started writing letters to groups of people in Italy, Greece and Turkey amongst other places. Later longer documents were written, and these were copied out carefully and passed from hand to hand. These are the writings that make up the *New Testament* and the person they are all about – is Jesus.

The longest four documents give us eye-witness accounts of his life, and most of the others are written to groups of people who had come to believe that Jesus was the Son of God who had made it possible for everybody to know their Creator as a personal heavenly father.

These writings of the *New Testament*, together with the *Old Testament*, make up what we call the *Holy Bible*. The Old Testament part of the Bible contains books which tell in one way or another the history of a remarkable nation – the Jews. Centuries before the birth of Jesus the Jews were convinced that a real, living God existed and had chosen their nation for a special purpose. In several places in the Old Testament writings there are clues which suggest that a very special person from God would be born a Jew at some stage in history.

Jesus was a Jew – born in Bethlehem, a village some five miles south of Jerusalem. He was called *Christ* [meaning 'anointed one'] by those in his time and since who became sure that he was the special person from God mentioned in the Old Testament writings.

So we know, today, about Jesus from the pages of the

17

New Testament but we mustn't forget that the people who wrote those pages knew about Jesus because – in most cases – *they had met him for themselves.*

Now let us see what they say.

WHAT WE KNOW ABOUT JESUS

Strangely enough we don't begin with Jesus but with someone else who was, in fact, his cousin. His name was John and he became known as John the Baptist.

John was a rugged, 'tough guy' of a preacher who emerged from the deserts to startle the people who lived on the fertile banks of the river Jordan. He drew huge crowds to listen to what was an awe-inspiring message. He said that God's special person, 'The Lord', the 'Lamb of God', was about to come. People had to 'Prepare the way of the Lord' just as such ancient Jewish prophets as Isaiah had said. People had to admit they were wrongdoers and short of God's perfect standards and he called them to turn away from the wrong things in their lives.

And those who said that they wanted to do this were baptised. That means they waded into the river Jordan with John and let him push them under and pull them up again! It was a strange ceremony, but its meaning was clear. It pictured the washing away of the old life and the beginning of a new life with the old sins forgiven.

One day John saw Jesus, his cousin, wading towards him to be baptised and he tried to refuse. His reason is important – *he believed that Jesus was the special one from God that he had been preaching about. Jesus didn't need to be forgiven.*

STRANGE EVENTS

John probably knew this because his mother had told him about the strange events leading up to and surrounding the birth of his cousin. It was known in the family that although his aunt Mary was the mother of Jesus, his uncle Joseph was not the father. There was no human father. Mary had been told in a vision she was going to give birth to 'The Son of the Most High God' before she and Joseph married.[1]

The 'Christmas story' is well known to us – perhaps too well known. It will do us no harm to go over the ground again.

Shortly after the marriage the baby was born while Joseph and Mary were in Bethlehem to report for a Government census – a sort of national head count. Bethlehem was crowded out. The only place they could find to stay in was a stable attached to the village inn. Jesus was born in that stable, and his first cradle was an animal trough.

Then came the visitors. First on the night the baby was born a crowd of over-excited shepherds burst into the stable with a strange story. They said that angels had come to them in the fields and told them that 'Christ the Lord' had been born and that they were to go to the village where they would find him lying – in a feeding trough! And that's just what they did.

Then, some time later, a group of foreign noblemen arrived with the sorts of gifts that young princes would be given. They insisted on giving their gifts to Jesus. His birth, they said, had been marked by a strange new star in the skies.

Soon after the noblemen left, Joseph, Mary's husband, had a dream warning him to get Mary and the baby out of Bethlehem. He did so. Shortly afterwards soldiers burst into Bethlehem sent by the corrupt King Herod. They were looking for the child the noblemen had visited. They asked no questions. They merely butchered every male child under two years of age, hoping that one of them would be Jesus.

1. Luke 1:32

19

MEANWHILE – BACK AT THE RIVER

John the Baptist probably knew all these stories and others. He was sure that Jesus was 'the Son of the Most High' – the special one who was to come. As such, Jesus had no sins to repent of and no need of Baptism. But Jesus persuaded him to go ahead and when it happened a voice was heard from heaven saying: 'You are my own dear Son. I am pleased with you.'[2]

JESUS THE TEACHER

As soon as he left the river Jordan Jesus walked away into the nearby desert. Over some five or six weeks he was nowhere to be seen and then, as his cousin had done, he came out of the desert with a message for the people.

He was very different from John – quieter and less dramatic but what he said was more astonishing to the ears of his listeners. The religious teachers of that time always quoted wise writers of past days and discussed their opinions. But Jesus kept saying: '*I* tell you'. The one thing that stood out a mile was this quiet note of absolute authority and sureness.

But Jesus went beyond this. People gasped as he would say that he had the power to forgive sins. 'How does he dare to talk like this?' spluttered pious hearers. 'God is the only one who can forgive sins!'[3] But Jesus said it and meant it.

Much of his teaching was in gentle stories. Stories that stuck in the mind, rang bells with people and yet often left them puzzled. He talked about a Lord who held a great feast and none of his guests wanted to come. But who was the Lord? And what was the feast? He didn't say.

He talked about a man stumbling across treasure in a

2. Luke 3:22
3. Mark 2:7

field and who sold everything to be able to buy the field. But what was the treasure meant to be? He talked about a man deeply in debt who had been let off but who would not overlook the tiny debts to him of one of his friends. What was the big debt? He talked about people who rented a farm and who killed the owner's son when he came for the rent. Who was the owner? Why did the son have to be killed?

And there were many more of these stories or parables.

JESUS CALLS FOLLOWERS

As Jesus went about teaching he called together a group of close followers – men like Simon Peter, Andrew, and the brothers James and John (whose outbursts earned them, from Jesus, the nicknames of 'Sons of Thunder'). One of those who followed Jesus was called Judas Iscariot. It was Judas who was later to plot the downfall of his Master.

Jesus began to concentrate his time and his teaching on this inner group. It was as if he was training them to take over from him. Somehow he seemed to know that he hadn't long to live.

PLOTS

And he was right. From the earliest days of his travelling and teaching, people were joining together to plot his arrest and, if possible, death sentence. In spite of the fact that Jesus taught comforting things (such as that Almighty God could be a personal loving Father to everyone) people took offence. They did not like the way that Jesus showed up their religion to be self-centred and all a big act. When Jesus performed miracles of healing his growing group of critics suggested that this was because of evil power, and they protested whenever he had *worked* the miracles on what was supposed to be a holy day of rest – the Sabbath.

The strongest religious group in Judea was called the

Sadducees. They talked about God but didn't believe in the supernatural and life after death. They were anxious about keeping in favour with the Roman authorities and they were very worried about the large crowd who mobbed Jesus almost everywhere he went. They feared that his followers would either become a mob revolting against Roman rule; or cause the Romans to fear a revolt, which was just as dangerous.

The rivals to the Sadducees were the Pharisees. In previous years they had taken heroic stands for the principles they believed in. But by the time of Jesus they had become very narrow-minded. They were more interested in keeping strictly to a set of rules than seeing people being healed and finding happiness through what Jesus said and did.

Normally the Sadducees and Pharisees hated each other. But they joined forces, together with another group known as the Herodians, to try to stop Jesus.

JESUS BETRAYED

Their great moment came during the Passover celebrations in the capital city of Jerusalem. Jesus and his followers arrived along with the hundreds of pilgrims. Very quickly Jesus was to be found as a teacher amongst those flocking in and out of the temple. The plotters sent people to try to trip him up and make him say something that would turn the crowds against him. But they found Jesus gently and firmly caught out those who were sent to catch him out! It only added more interest and spice to the teaching sessions that Jesus held.

Then came something that the plotters never thought possible. Judas Iscariot went to see them and for the promise of a handsome fee offered to lead them to a place where Jesus would be away from excited followers who might rally to his defence. Late one evening Judas led the soldiers out to a lonely spot outside Jerusalem and the arrest took place.

The band of followers who were with Jesus at the time left him and ran for their lives.

There followed a hastily arranged trial which led to Jesus being declared guilty of blasphemy (of setting himself up as God.) The punishment for this would normally have been death but as Judea was now a Roman colony the sentence had to be agreed by the Roman governor, Pontius Pilate. Pilate interviewed the prisoner and felt deeply uneasy. He had proved to be a callous and cruel man in the past but he desperately tried to have Jesus either released or punished by flogging and then released.

THE CROWDS AGAINST JESUS

By then rumours were sweeping the crowds in Jerusalem. The plotters had planted people throughout the city to stir up the crowds against Jesus. They crowded round the Governor's Palace on the verge of rioting and chanted for Jesus to be crucified. Crucifixion – nailing a man up on a tree or stake and leaving him to die – was a particularly horrible way of execution that the Romans used when dealing with the most dangerous criminals.

Pilate gave in to stop the possibility of a riot but he refused to take the responsibility for the death sentence. Jesus was led away and crucified.

*　　*　　*

This, then, is an outline of the Christ of Christianity. A remarkable man from a humble background who got into trouble with the powerful people of his time and was arrested and put to death.

It hardly seems important enough to set off the world-wide religion that has survived for centuries and even in this century is growing by leaps and bounds in some parts of the world. How has *Christianity* grown out of this man Jesus?

I believe there can only be one answer, *and that is in the part of the story I haven't told*.

In the New Testament we have four accounts of the life of Jesus. They were written by different people at different times and in different places. Three of them were written by the original followers of Jesus, one of them was written by a Greek doctor who interviewed the eye-witnesses some time later. They all agree on the basic story we have just read. But they all agree – even though they differ on some small details – about something else.

They all agree that Jesus of Nazareth was laid in a tomb after his crucifixion and then within three days was clearly seen to be alive again by hundreds of his followers! What is more – the body of Jesus has never been found up to this day.

THE COWARDS BECOME BRAVE

The followers of Jesus who had been terrified by the chanting crowds when their leader was sentenced to death, changed in an amazing way. Within weeks they were standing up before those same crowds and declaring bravely that Jesus had been raised from the dead by his heavenly Father. This time people listened and hundreds began to put their faith in Jesus as Son of God and the one who saves men and women from their sins.

A LOAD OF OLD MYTHS?

Today as we look at this story we have to decide. Do we dismiss it as a load of old myths? Do we believe that those who wrote up those four accounts all got it wrong? (It's strange that they all got it wrong in the same way!)

Or do we say – 'This sounds important; we must find out as much as we can!' And there is certainly very much more to discover.

Questions

1. Where do we get our information about Jesus?
2. What did John's Baptism stand for?
3. Why didn't John want to baptise Jesus?
4. What was so different about the way Jesus taught?
5. Why was Jesus put to death?
6. Why do you think we are still talking about Jesus today?

The Creed

Think over the following part of the Apostles' Creed in the light of what you have read:

I believe ... in Jesus Christ his only Son our Lord, Who was conceived by the Holy Ghost, Born of the Virgin Mary, suffered under Pontius Pilate, was crucified, dead and buried: He descended into hell; The Third day he rose again from the dead; He ascended into heaven, And sitteth at the right hand of God the Father Almighty; From thence he will come to judge the quick and the dead.

Passages to Read

1. Matt. 3:1–17
2. Mark 8:27–30
3. Luke 23:32–49
4. John 20:19–29

3: Life with Father

Jesus taught that there is a God – in fact he claimed to have come into the world to show us what God is like. 'Whoever has seen me,' he said, 'has seen the Father ... I am in the Father and the Father is in me.'[1]

Amazing words – and notice the way he talks about God as *Father*. We shall be coming back to this later.

WHAT JESUS TOOK FOR GRANTED

But first we must see what Jesus took for granted about God. He was born into the Hebrew nation and the Hebrews had strong, clear beliefs about God. And Jesus said that those views were right as far as they went. Let me quickly point out some of the basic truths about God, which we can see from the Old Testament writings of the Hebrew people.

1. GOD IS BEFORE AND AFTER ALL THINGS. The opening words of the Bible are: 'In the beginning ... God ...'[2] The Jews never sat down to work out whether there was a God or not. They were convinced that the people who had written the Old Testament scriptures had met God in one way or another.

And they were convinced that he had always been and would always be. He was – as Moses discovered – the great 'I AM' of all time.

1. John 14:9, 11
2. Gen. 1:1

26

2. GOD IS CREATOR OF ALL THINGS. This is made very clear in the opening pages of the Bible. There we find the creation of the world looked at from two different angles. What stands out very clearly from those accounts is the careful, patient creation of a beautiful and complex world. God is pictured rather like a skilled craftsman, sitting back at the end of each phase of his work and checking that it is *good* (Gen. 1:10).

What is created is an unspoiled world, and the human race is created as the final work of art – we were made in the very likeness of God himself (Gen. 1:26). But there is a good reason for our 'specialness'. Men and women are meant to be God's deputies, looking after and caring for the wonderful world that has been given us. If the world is to 'work' properly, mankind must see that it is God's world, and look after it on God's behalf.

3. GOD CARES FOR INDIVIDUALS. The creator of the world however is someone who wants to be in touch with and guide individual people. People matter to this great, eternal God. So we read right through the Bible that he is able to get in touch with people. Abraham (Gen. 12) becomes absolutely convinced that the great I AM is telling him to move well away from his homeland and become the founder of a new and special nation. That nation, his descendants, was to be the Hebrew nation, and from it God promised blessing to all the nations of the world.

4. GOD CARES ABOUT JUSTICE. By the time we come to the second book of the Bible, *Exodus*, we read that the Hebrew nation has become a race of slaves within the boundaries of Egypt. We then see, through his dealings with Moses, that God cares about how nations treat each other. He is someone who is wrapped up in the affairs of the world he has created – and he is angry about those who bully and oppress others weaker than themselves.

Exodus tells us how the great I AM breaks into history

to rescue Abraham's descendants and sets them up as a nation in their own right.

5. GOD DEMANDS HOLY AND OBEDIENT LIVING. Having created the nation of Israel after the escape from Egypt, it is soon clear that God is not someone who goes in for favouritism. The Israelites are expected to obey God's commandments – the rules and guidelines for good living. When they become casual and careless about them, things begin to go wrong. God sets standards. He blesses those who try to keep them, and he turns his holy anger upon those who don't.

For the Jew, and therefore for Jesus himself, right and wrong, and good and bad were far more than matters of opinion. They were not fashions that were respected in one generation and forgotten in the next. Right and wrong and good and bad were to do with the unchanging will of an unchanging God. And to respect and honour the will of God was the best thing a man could do, and also the only way to find true happiness. 'Happy are those who follow his commands,' wrote the Psalmist.[3]

6. GOD IS IN CONTROL OF HISTORY. If you think about what I have been saying you will see that God is involved in the story of mankind. All through the pages of the Old Testament you will find this strong theme. God is working out his will in the world. But he is not doing it by putting everyone on puppet strings.

The amazing thing about Almighty God is that he can work out his will in the world without taking away our freedom to be real people able to choose for ourselves. A friend of mine used to say that God is like a master chess player. He can always bring about the result he wants in spite of what the opponent may be doing to bring about the opposite result!

And one cannot read the Old Testament without feeling

3. Ps. 119:2

that everything is leading up to something big. And that something big – was the coming of the Son of God into time and space. The letter to the Hebrews opens with some words that show how God's son, Jesus, fits into all we have been considering:

> In the past, God spoke to our ancestors many times and in many ways through the prophets, but in these last days he has spoken to us through his Son.[4]

GOD WANTS TO SPEAK TO MEN

The Maker of the world, who creates and judges nations and whose standards of right and wrong last forever, is a God who longs to talk with men and women! This is the message that jumps out of the Bible. It is why Jesus came.

The Christian doesn't believe in God because he's thought it out as a sort of intellectual exercise. We talk with certainty about God, *because he has spoken to us and shown us what he is like*. And Jesus is the chief speaker and revealer of God's nature.

GOD CAN BE 'OUR FATHER'

Now here is something that I find exciting! If we flick through the pages of the Old Testament we will hardly ever find God being spoken of as a *Father*. There are just a handful of places where someone catches a glimpse of this truth.

But turn to the New Testament and what do we find? Why – the word 'Father' is on practically every page (and there are a lot of pages!). This is the startling change that Jesus has brought.

All that is spoken of God in the Old Testament is true. But as well as being the awesome and great I AM, our God wants us to look to him as 'Our Father'. And Jesus stressed

4. Heb. 1:1, 2

this by sometimes using the Hebrew word for 'daddy' – '*abba*'. Our great God, can be our personal heavenly Father – our daddy!

BECOMING GOD'S CHILDREN

Notice that I say 'can be' our Father. Jesus did not teach that God is the Father of everyone and therefore that all men are brothers. This bond with him and with each other depends on how we react to Jesus himself.

In John's gospel this is made clear. Looking back on the earthly days of Jesus and all the opposition that the Lord met John writes:

> Some, however, did receive him and believed in him; so he gave them the right to become God's children.[5]

It is when you and I welcome Jesus into our lives and put our trust in him and in what he is all about that a change takes place in how we stand in God's sight, and a change takes place with regard to others who are Christians.

Life, for the Christian, is life with Father in a family of brothers and sisters.

BELIEVING IN GOD THE FATHER

We have thought through a few basic things about God. There is far more to say about him, but we had to limit ourselves because of space. Let me close by sharing with you something of what it means to me to believe in the God Jesus revealed.

1. I KNOW THAT I AM MEANT TO BE. Because I believe in a God who created the world and all that is in it; and because I believe that this God is working out his purposes – *I know that I matter*. I am not an accident. There is a purpose for me being around!

5. John 1:12

And it doesn't matter *how* God made the world; whether it was suddenly, as some Christians understand the Bible, or whether it was through some process of evolution as other Christians believe. What matters is that the great I AM is behind the fact that you and I *are!* We are *wanted!*

2. I KNOW I AM LOVED. You cannot read the Bible and miss this fact. God didn't make the world and forget about it. Making me is a sign that he cares about me. And coming in Jesus to show us how to live, and to die to take the blame for our sins (more about that later) all this shouts at us that God is love!

3. I KNOW THAT THERE REALLY ARE SUCH THINGS AS RIGHT AND WRONG, GOOD AND BAD. Life can be very confusing if we don't have standards and goals. Worse than that – it can become chaos. But God has shown us where he stands and what he wants from men in the way they live. I find this a great comfort – even if those standards seem beyond reach. (And more about this later, as well.)

4. I CAN SEE THAT THE WORLD IS MEANT TO BE LOOKED AFTER. In recent years there has been growing interest in what is called *ecology* – the whole science of realising that the world is a delicate, precision system that needs looking after. But I learn this from the opening pages of the Bible. So I see part of my duty in life is to preserve the earth, which in its own turn preserves me!

5. I BELIEVE WHAT IS RIGHT WILL WIN IN THE END. God made a good world and God is working through history, and God is forever, and God is just. All this means, for me, that what is good and right is what will remain at the end of time. And I am the Father's child – I believe I shall be around to see the final victory of what is right!

So I am not too depressed at the many wrong things I see around me (and in me). Like the master chess player, the Father will end up getting the result he wants!

6. I BELONG TO A NEW FAMILY. God is my Father, and

other Christians are my brothers and sisters. I belong to a new, world-wide forever family.

It's nice to belong to something good!

Questions
1. Why do Christians think of God as a heavenly Father?
2. What is the job which God has given the human race to do?
3. How do we know what God is like?

The Creed
Think over the following part of the Apostles' Creed in the light of what you have read:

> I believe in God, the Father Almighty, Maker of heaven and earth.

Passages to Read
1. Genesis chapters 1 and 2
   (This looks in simple terms at the creation story from two different angles.)
2. Acts 17:16–31
3. Luke 11:1–13

4: The Rebel Race

Open any day's newspaper and on practically every page one thing stands out. There's a great deal wrong with the human race!

Think over what you have done in the past year of your life and one thing sticks out like a sore finger: your own life is far from perfect. If the world was made up of people exactly like yourself, what would it be like? The chances are that it would be just like the world you read about in any day's newspaper!

So we're back where we started. What has got into us all?

WHAT DID JESUS SAY?

Jesus put over much of his teaching by means of stories. These stories, or parables as they are called, were often puzzling, but they were all extremely memorable.

My favourite parable is the one we call the story of the *Prodigal Son*. It is in fact a bad title because the real hero of the story is the Father – and yes, you've guessed it: *the Father is a picture of God*. However the story is full of meaning and has a great deal to say not only about the nature of God but also about the nature of men and women. I want to concentrate here on the first part of the story.

Here's how it goes:

Jesus went on to say, 'There was once a man who had two sons. The younger one said to him, "Father, give me my share of the property now." So the man divided his property between his two sons. After a few days the younger son sold his part of the property and left home with the money. He went to a country far away, where he wasted his money in reckless living. He spent everything he had. Then a severe famine spread over that country, and he was left without a thing. So he went to work for one of the citizens of that country, who sent him out to his farm to take care of the pigs. He wished he could fill himself with the bean pods the pigs ate, but no one gave him anything to eat. At last he came to his senses and said, "All my father's hired workers have more than they can eat, and here I am about to starve! I will get up and go to my father and say, 'Father, I have sinned against God and against you. I am no longer fit to be called your son; treat me as one of your hired workers.'" So he got up and started back to his father.

'He was still a long way from home when his father saw him; his heart was filled with pity, and he ran, threw his arms round his son, and kissed him. "Father," the son said, "I have sinned against God and against you. I am no longer fit to be called your son." But the father called his servants. "Hurry!" he said. "Bring the best robe and put it on him. Put a ring on his finger and shoes on his feet. Then go and get the prize calf and kill it, and let us celebrate with a feast! For this son of mine was dead, but now he is alive; he was lost, but now he has been found." And so the feasting began.'[1]

IMPATIENT

The first thing we see is that the son was impatient to run his own affairs. He wanted to be king of his own

1. Luke 15:11–24

castle. *'Give me ... now!'* is his cry. The set-up was one where he worked under his father's leadership and was going to inherit plenty of power and possessions later on – but that was not enough.

Now this is exactly the sort of picture we find in the Creation stories in the book of Genesis. There the first man and woman are described as the keepers of their heavenly Father's garden. They are under the Creator's leadership. But the temptation comes to them to 'be like God' so they rebel, take charge, and do what they want to do.[2]

If we follow Jesus's story through, we see that the rebel son has a great deal of pleasure out of his freedom but ends in a desperate mess. His wealth has gone, the place where he lives is in the grip of famine and he wishes he could be given even pig food to eat but 'no one gave him any'. What a contrast! The story starts with the son demanding 'Give me', and leads to a situation where no one gives him anything. *Putting oneself first looks fine until we see what it is like when everyone else is putting themselves first!*

A PICTURE OF OUR WORLD

It is very hard not to feel that this simple story is a picture of our world. Human self-centredness lies at the heart of wars, famines (in a world where many have plenty), injustice, class-strife and so on. Many a Sunday School teacher has pointed out that in our British word 'sin', the 'I' is at the centre of things! It's a helpful coincidence!

No football team could get very far if every player (no matter how good) played with the 'I' at the centre of things. Yet our world is meant to be a massive complex team of nations and people – and we are all trying to live with the 'I' at the centre of things! The prophecy in the book of Isaiah puts it in these terms:

2. Gen. 3:4, 5

All of us were like sheep that were lost, each of us going his own way.[3]

WHY DIDN'T THE FATHER STOP HIM?

The boy tells his father that he wants to break free. So what does the father do? *He lets him go.* There are no arguments and no pleading. He sees that the boy's mind is made up. It is clear that the Father does not try to force his son to do what he doesn't want to do – *even though the boy is in the wrong.* The father is not prepared to rule unless his rule is wanted.

Here again the picture fits in with the creation story. We read about the tree with forbidden fruit in the Garden of Eden. If that tree with its tempting fruit had not been there, then there would have been no trouble. But there would have been no real freedom either!

The truth is clear from both these passages in the Bible – *God would rather have persons than puppets*; but this means that a rebellion can always happen. So even though the father probably realised his boy would make a mess of things, he lets him go rather than force him to stay.

GOD'S ANGER

But the father doesn't help the son make the mess. He stays at home and keeps well away. And this point is important. It is one thing for God to allow all of us to be free enough to make a mess of our lives but it is quite a different thing to expect him to approve of the mess. The father in Jesus's story keeps away from his son and therefore keeps away from all that his son does.

This is what is meant by God's judgment. We often think of judgment as if it was God coming in with a big stick. The truth is that God is love and his way of judging is usually to keep his loving, protecting, helpful self away from us

3. Isa. 53:6

36

when we are in the wrong. The prophet Habakkuk, whose words are found in the Old Testament said that God's 'eyes are too holy to look at evil'.[4] St. Paul in his letter to Christians in Rome put it more strongly. In a section where he writes about God's holy anger at the sins and rebellion of men and women he three times uses the words: 'God has given them over.'[5] What he means is that God shows his anger by standing back and letting us get on with the mess that we are all making.

Why doesn't he come closer? Because that would be going back to forcing us to act against our wills. Rather the hope is that all of us will come to realise that we need the Father's help and company again.

That's what happened to the rebel son in the story we have been considering. We read: 'At last he came to his senses and said ... "I will get up and go to my Father." '

From this we can see the sort of anger and judgment that belongs to our heavenly Father. It has a kindness and gentleness about it! It is God's way both of telling us off, and of giving us a chance to 'come to our senses' and to change our minds of our own free will!

WELCOME HOME!

So the rebel son swallows his pride and turns for home. As he tramps along he rehearses his little speech of apology. All he is going to ask for is a job on the farm. There will be no talk of being a member of the family any more, or of having a share in the family farming business. It's a great come-down but much better than starving. Head down he marches on.

And what happens? While 'he was still a long way from home ... his father saw him; his heart was filled with pity

4. Hab. 1:13
5. Rom. 1:24, 26, 28

and he ran, threw his arms round his son, and kissed him.'
The boy tries to make his little speech and to ask for a job,
but his father won't let him finish. All he is bothered about
is that his once rebellious son has no shoes and is covered
in rags. The son wants a job, the father calls for a party. The
son hopes to become a servant. The father rejoices to
welcome home – his son.

I think it's a marvellous story that speaks so vividly of
the forgiveness of God. No matter how much we may have
rebelled and no matter how much we may belong to a rebel
race – our heavenly Father comes to meet us as soon as we
make up our minds to go home to him. The story is about
sin – yes. But it is even more about forgiveness.

A SPIRITUAL BATTLE

But a story – even one from Jesus – cannot tell us
everything, and the parables were never meant to put
over everything there is to know. The teaching of the
Bible makes clear that our sin and the sinfulness of all
men is part of an immense spiritual battle. St. Paul
wrote:

> We are not fighting against human beings but against
> the wicked spiritual forces in the heavenly world, the
> rulers, the authorities, and cosmic powers of this dark
> age.[6]

The writers of the Bible did not go into great detail but
they clearly believed that there is an evil one – Satan or the
Devil. In the story of the Garden of Eden we read that the
temptation to disobey God and to be 'like gods' came to
Adam and Eve from what is described as 'the serpent'.
Jesus himself, we read in the fourth chapter of both Matthew and Luke's gospels, was put under great testing and
temptation by the Devil. We read of Jesus meeting people

6. Eph. 6:12

38

possessed by evil spirits and casting out these evil spirits. Many people reject such stories by saying that the people who wrote up the life and teachings of Jesus were simple and superstitious. They say that Jesus was dealing with people who were mentally ill perhaps, but certainly not demon-possessed.

But it is not quite so easy to say these passages were written by people who didn't understand about mental illness. Anyone who has travelled throughout the world soon discovers that in every continent one can still meet cases of something a bit more worrying than mental illness. Indeed in modern Western countries, as well as those lands where witch doctors can still be found, there are plenty of cases where many doctors admit they can bring no cures or prescribe no treatments.

BEWARE!

There is a whole area of life which could be called 'spiritual' but which is dangerous. No person should be foolish enough to play games with tumblers and ouiji boards, or to dabble with fortune telling, magic, spiritualism, or any of those activities which go under the name of the occult. Beware and keep clear – what can start as a game can end in terrible distress!

If what we have just been considering seems rather frightening it is important to see that there is no need for any fear. St. Paul wrote: 'There is nothing in all creation that will ever be able to separate us from the love of God which is ours through Christ Jesus our Lord.'[7] If we are truly wanting to follow Jesus in our daily lives then we will be kept safe from any evil. Jesus taught us to pray 'deliver us from evil'. He did that to keep us well aware of the danger but also to remind us that he is a deliverer and protector.

7. Rom. 8:39

FINAL JUDGMENT

But to return to the story of the rebel son. What if he had not 'come to his senses' and returned home? The answer must surely be that he would have lost for ever the love and help of his father.

Jesus taught that this is what could happen to any man or woman who deliberately stays a rebel to his heavenly Father. He talked of Hell, or outer darkness or everlasting fire. He said that, after death, someone who hadn't turned back to the Father would continue to exist in the same sort of way as smouldering rubbish existed in the dump outside of a big city – unwanted and rejected.

If this is so then it is clear that we must take our own rebellion against God very, very seriously. Obviously Jesus was using picture language to describe Hell, but the point is that these are horrible pictures. How much more lovely is the picture of a father running down the road to welcome the son who has decided to come home!

Some people are put off by this talk of Hell. They cannot believe that a God of love would send anyone to such a fate. But the truth is that if we end up in such a 'place', *it is because we sent ourselves there* because we were people who wanted nothing to do with our heavenly Father. Hell is just another way of describing the state of things where there is no contact with a loving God who is the source of all beauty and goodness.

Questions
1. What was the beginning of the Prodigal son's troubles?
2. Why didn't the father try to stop him – and what is the lesson for us to learn?
3. In what way is God's anger actually kind to us?
4. How do people end up in what is called Hell?

Passages to Read

1. Gen. 3
2. Matt. 18:21–35
3. Rom. 1:18–32
4. Rev. 20:11–15 with John 5:24

For Further Thought

Read and think over the section in the Appendix at the back of this book on the Ten Commandments. Notice how God's laws are about what will make life better for all of us.

5: The Death that brought New Life

Perhaps some of the most surprising words anyone has ever written are these:

> As for me, however, I will boast only about the cross of our Lord Jesus Christ ...[1]

The words were written by St. Paul, the great Christian teacher and traveller of the first century. Perhaps you don't see them as very odd so let me suggest how the meaning of those words would be today:

> The thing that I am proud about is that the Lord Jesus Christ went to the firing squad!

Now we might think this made sense if St. Paul was anti-Jesus. But we know he was one of Jesus Christ's greatest followers. So why was he so pleased about his hero's execution?

THE SYMBOL OF CHRISTIANITY

Nor is St. Paul alone in this odd way of thinking about the death of Jesus. The best known symbol of Christianity

1. Gal. 6:14

which you will find in practically every Church – is the cross, which was the equivalent in Roman times of the gallows or electric chair.

It seems that the death of Jesus is at least as important as his life! *And Jesus thought so as well.*

WHAT JESUS SAID

If you read the accounts of Jesus's life written in the gospels of Mark and Matthew, and read them carefully, you will see that a very important point in the story is reached when Peter realises who Jesus is. 'You are the Messiah,' he says, 'the Son of the Living God.'[2]

Up to that point in the story we see those first followers of Jesus excited and yet puzzled by the amazing man they are with. Then it dawns on Peter. This is no ordinary man! This is the Messiah! The one the Jews had long believed would come amongst them and bring about a tremendous act of God! Jesus, Peter could see, was not just another prophet or teacher.

Now look what Jesus does:

From that time on Jesus began to say plainly to his disciples, 'I must go to Jerusalem and suffer much from the elders, the chief priests, and the teachers of the Law. I will be put to death, but three days later I will be raised to life.'[3]

Peter and the others didn't like this, but it is clear that from the moment they saw that Jesus was special, Jesus began to teach them that his death was important.

So we can say this: *if we are to understand Jesus properly we must understand why he died and what that death means.*

2. Matt. 16:16
3. Matt. 16:21, 22

43

WHY DID JESUS DIE?

From one point of view the reason for the death of Jesus is clear – he died because he was arrested, tried and sentenced to death.

This is certainly true. As Jesus went around teaching and healing he made many enemies. We thought earlier of the two great Jewish religious groups, the Pharisees and the Sadducees. Jesus so upset both of them that although they usually hated each other, they worked together to have him arrested.

So Jesus was arrested, tried, pronounced guilty, sentenced to death and crucified.

All this is surely a tragedy. But St. Paul saw the cross as a victory and something to cheer about. Why was this? Jesus himself gave the answer.

On the same night that he was arrested Jesus had brought his disciples together to eat the traditional Passover supper. The Passover supper was a meal which had a great deal of meaning built into it. It was an occasion when a Jewish family would think together about the great rescue act of God when he had caused the Israelites to escape from the Egyptians in the times of Moses. It was a solemn meal that spoke of a great victory brought about by God.

But Jesus changed the message built into that ancient meal. He made it speak of a new rescue act of God for those who were his followers. Here is how someone present at that 'Last Supper' wrote about it:

While they were eating, Jesus took a piece of bread, gave a prayer of thanks, broke it, and gave it to his disciples. 'Take and eat it,' he said; 'this is my body.' Then he took a cup, gave thanks to God, and gave it to them. 'Drink it, all of you,' he said; 'this is my blood which seals God's covenant, my blood poured out for many for the forgiveness of sins.'[4]

It is quite clear from these words that Jesus saw his death as the way by which God could rescue us from the great tyranny of our sins. His blood was 'poured out for many for the forgiveness of sins'.

SACRIFICE

Obviously what we have here is the idea of *sacrifice*. All through the Old Testament we can read about the various types of sacrifices that the Jewish religion carried out. The taking of an animal's life was linked to the confessing and admitting of people's sins. In this way God made people see very clearly that sins were far more serious than little imperfections. They were terrible blots in our lives that distressed a Holy God and brought sad and bad things into our world.

But the sacrifices of the Old Testament didn't actually *earn* the forgiveness they brought. When you have read the Bible carefully for some time you will realise that those Old Testament sacrifices were no more than poor *copies* of the one and only sacrifice that could possibly deal with our sins – and that sacrifice was the death of Jesus.

The writer of the letter to the Hebrews saw this very clearly. Jesus, he wrote, was the High Priest of all time offering the one and only sacrifice that could put everyone right with God. But he was more – he was also the very sacrifice itself! And the sacrifice of himself that he offered was much better than the Jewish temple sacrifices. As a result, he said, the problem of our sins has been well and truly dealt with. Here is one of the key passages in the letter which makes this point:

4. Matt. 26:26–29

The Jewish High Priest goes into the Most Holy Place every year with the blood of an animal. But Christ did not go in to offer himself many times . . . Instead . . . he has appeared once and for all . . . to remove sin through the sacrifice of himself.[5]

Let us sum up what we have seen so far.
Jesus died because:
1. Men arrested and killed him
              and
2. God meant him to be a sacrifice for our sins.

BUT WHY A SACRIFICE?

'But just a moment,' some people say. 'Why do we have to think about such a nasty idea as a sacrifice? If God loves us why doesn't he just go ahead and forgive us?'

This is a good question. There are many people who find the idea of Jesus as a sacrifice a horrid one. They say it makes Christianity into a 'butcher-shop religion'. Others feel that it makes God out to be a brutal, bloodthirsty being who has got to be revenged on someone for our sins before he can let us off. People who talk in this way and raise these objections are often very sincere in what they are saying, so we must take their objections seriously.

Why then, cannot God simply forgive us our sins and let it go at that?

The answer to this is that God has to be true to himself – and he *hates* sin. And may I say; it's a very good thing that he does! If we want a God who overlooks sin and hands out forgiveness without being concerned about sin; *then we are wanting a God who has no standards and who sets us no example to live by*.

If God has standards then this encourages *us* to have standards. If we know that God wants fair dealings and has

5. Heb. 9:25, 26

no favourites, it encourages us to treat other people fairly, but if God has standards then how is he to show them? Surely by making clear before men what he is pleased with, and also what displeases him.

But how does he show his displeasure? Do we want him to say 'tut tut' and then leave it at that? Such a course of action wouldn't deserve much respect from us. No, if God has standards and he 'draws the line' about what is good and bad, then we should expect to *see him showing himself to be the enemy of what is bad*.

And the only way he can do this properly is to turn his back on what he finds displeasing and below standard. That makes the matter clear and beyond doubt.

But the problem is that *we are all below God's standards*. The reason that the world we live in is so wrong in so many ways is that it is full of people like ourselves. So what is God to do about *us*?

And this is God's big problem – a problem that can be set out in two phrases:

1. He loves sinners therefore he wants to be near them.
2. He hates sin therefore he must have nothing to do with sinners.

HOW TO BE AGAINST SIN BUT *FOR* SINNERS

So the big problem which faces our Creator is this – how to be clearly seen to be *against* sin and yet *for* those of us who are sinners. To put it another way – how can God clearly keep his standards, and yet be a father and friend to those who fall way below them – which means you and I?

The answer that he chose showed his amazing mercy and kindness for us all. He decided to show in public his rejection of all that stands for sin and to do it in such a way that it didn't involve us. He put the blame for your sins and mine on Jesus and showed that he was turning his back on

Jesus because Jesus was standing in for all sinners.

St. Paul described it in these words:

> Christ was without sin, but for our sake God made him share our sins in order that in union with him we might share the righteousness of God.[6]

Now we must remember that Jesus and God the Father are very much closer than any father and son we will ever know. On one occasion Jesus went so far as to say: 'The Father and I are one.'[7] So the Father was deeply involved *on* the cross of Jesus. There is a sense in which we would be right to say: *God did not want to blame us for our sins so he took it out on himself.*

So the forgiveness that God our heavenly Father offers us was terribly costly to him – how we should treasure it! This is what the cross of Jesus has done.

1. It has allowed God to be clearly seen as a just God who does not lower his standards.
2. It has allowed God to be able to deal with us as if we were just also.

And if you read Rom. 3:25–26 carefully you will find that Paul is saying exactly that. No wonder he felt that the cross of Jesus was something to boast about!

SO MUCH MORE TO SAY

No chapter on the cross, indeed no book about it, would ever say all there was to say. I believe the cross of Jesus will always have new meanings and say new things to us.

However the first thing to say always is that Jesus, by dying for us, has brought us forgiveness; and if he had not died for us – we could not be forgiven. No matter how hard it may be to understand why Jesus died – God wants all men to know that truth.

6. 2 Cor. 5:21
7. John 10:30

48

But there are other things to say and I will simply mention one of them. The cross sets us an example. It is the example of someone who refused to strike back at those who struck out so unfairly at him. He did not add to the total of violent things that were done on the day he died. His way of victory was not that of beating down other people or hitting back. He suffered patiently, knowing that God himself would put things right and turn what looked like defeat into victory.

And God did that in a tremendous way – as we shall see in the next chapter!

Questions
1. Why do you think that the cross has become one of the great symbols of Christianity?
2. What was the meaning that Jesus read into the Passover supper? In what way was it similar to the original meaning of the meal?
3. What is the big difference between the old Jewish sacrifices and the sacrifice of Jesus?
4. Why couldn't God 'just' forgive us our sins?
5. If Jesus has brought us forgiveness – do we have to do anything ourselves to receive it?

Passages to Read
1. Compare Isa. 53:5, 6, with 1 Pet. 2:24, 25
2. Mark 15:33–39
3. Rom. 3:22–26
4. Phil. 2:5–11

6: The Defeat of Death

If there had been newspapers at the time when it happened the headlines on the news stands would probably have looked like this:

IS JESUS ALIVE AGAIN?
— rumours sweep the city

EMPTY TOMB SENSATION!
— was body stolen or has a dead man risen?

BODY OF JESUS 'STOLEN'
— official statement by High Priest

What are we saying here? Simply that within three days of the body of Jesus being placed in a Jerusalem tomb, the grave was found to be empty and Jesus's friends were saying he was alive again.

Were they lying or telling the truth? This is the most important question we can ever ask. If they were lying we can forget about the whole business of Christianity. If they were telling the truth – everything is different for all of us!

WHAT HAPPENED TO THE CORPSE?

First of all let me make this clear – Jesus truly *died* on the cross. He was pronounced dead by those people who were in business to kill people – Roman soldiers. Just to make sure, the corpse was speared in the side before it was taken off the scaffold. The body was then wrapped tightly in cloth wrappings and placed in a cold damp cell. That is what we read in the nineteenth chapter of John's Gospel and it is backed up by the records of Luke, Mark and Matthew. The burial took place on the Friday evening. By Sunday morning there could have been no possibility of a spark of life in that corpse.

It is important to see this clearly, for every now and again someone suggests that Jesus didn't really die on the cross but merely fainted. Such people suggest that Jesus later revived in the coolness of the tomb. But the shock, the thirst, the loss of blood, the spear-wound, plus the bitter chill of the tomb make it certain that Jesus was dead.

And if he had – by some unlikely freak – survived he would have had to cope with being bound up in cloth wrappings almost like an Egyptian 'mummy', and then he would have had to roll away a huge boulder and chase off the guards who were camped on the entrance.

No – he was dead all right. So what happened?

While the Gospels writers Matthew, Mark, Luke and John don't agree on all the points of detail, they tell the same story. The burial of Jesus had been hurried through before the Friday evening. That was because the solemn Sabbath day of rest began at nightfall on the Friday and lasted until nightfall on the Saturday. In the rush there were various parts of the treatment of the corpse that had been left over until after the Sabbath. The next chance for the women to go to the tomb and finish treating the corpse was daybreak on the Sunday.

A group of women set out first thing on Sunday morning and when they got to the tomb there were no soldiers, the huge stone which had been pushed across the entrance was rolled back – and the body was gone.

Shortly after this the women in frantic excitement told a group of Jesus's leading followers what they had found plus the fact that they had met two strange men 'in bright

51

shining clothes' who were at the empty tomb and who told them that Jesus was alive again.

The menfolk were true to form on hearing this – they said the women were talking rubbish! Especially as at least one of the women, Mary of Magdala, actually claimed she had spoken briefly with Jesus himself.

Two leading disciples, John and Peter, ran to the tomb. They found it empty and there were no soldiers. What they did see however were the grave clothes. They were still there. And years afterwards John could remember the odd way the clothes were lying – almost as if they had crumpled flat as the body had vanished *from inside*.

Nobody – guard or disciple – actually saw Jesus walk out of the tomb. It seems that by the time the stone was rolled away – there was no body inside!

IMPOSSIBLE

Of course there is no natural explanation for this and that is why many non-Christians can't accept the facts as they appear. For the same reason some people who would call themselves Christians try to find other explanations for this amazing story because they want to protect Christianity from being rejected by intelligent people as 'too fantastic to take seriously'.

But I believe that no other explanation fits the facts. Some very good people have suggested that the descriptions of the rising of Jesus are not meant to be taken as historical fact but as true ideas expressed in a poetic way. The truth they would tell us is that while Jesus was physically dead his spirit and presence somehow lived on to inspire his followers.

Well, they have some truth here – the Spirit of Jesus does live on and we can all meet up with Jesus as he comes to us in the Holy Spirit. We shall be thinking about this in a later chapter. But the disciples who preached about the Holy

Spirit *did not say that this was the same thing as the raising of the body of Jesus*. And they insisted that the body of Jesus was nowhere to be found on earth.

And, indeed, no one to this day has ever found it. It wasn't long before the disciples were standing up in the city of Jerusalem and shouting their heads off about the rising of Jesus. The people who had put Jesus to death were the most powerful people in the city. They had to silence those disciples if they possibly could and the obvious way to shut them up was to produce the body.

They never did, because the body of Jesus was nowhere to be found.

STOLEN?

What the enemies of Jesus did do was to put about the story that the disciples had stolen the body.

Could this have been the case? Let's think about it for a moment. To say those men had stolen the body is to say that they were strong enough to overcome armed guards. Perhaps they could have done – but it hardly seems to be the sort of thing that a group of men would do who had just proved themselves to be weak and cowardly.

But not only do they become suddenly very brave and powerful – they become deceivers and liars. St. Paul some years later pointed this out himself, 'if Christ had not been raised from death,' he said, '... we are shown to be lying against God.'

But if we say that these men did suddenly become deceivers and liars we find ourselves having some very difficult questions to answer.

1. HOW DID THEY MANAGE TO HIDE THE BODY? It would have been very difficult to smuggle the body away and harder still to hide it. There were powerful people with everything to gain from finding that body. But they didn't.

2. WHAT DID THEY GAIN FROM THEIR LYING? People tell

lies when they want to gain something or escape from trouble. If the disciples turned into liars then they must have done it knowing they would lose everything (even their lives) from so doing. Far from escaping trouble they walked right into it. And they must have known this.

3. WHY DID THEY MAKE THEIR MESSAGE HARDER? The first Christians set out to share the message about Jesus. Right at the centre of their message was this claim that Jesus had risen again. The idea of God being interested in our bodies (apart from our souls) was one that the Greek-influenced people of those days could never understand. It wasn't only fantastic. They thought it was stupid! If these disciples wanted to win the world to their side why didn't they invent a message easier to believe?

HARD TO BELIEVE

No – the truth is that once you look closely at the facts, the story of the empty tomb and the risen Jesus becomes harder to disbelieve than to believe!

LIKE SCIENCE FICTION ONLY REAL!

But we must notice that the body was changed in some amazing way. Jesus did not sit up, shake off his wrappings and walk out of his tomb. God completely removed the body from the tomb leaving the clothes lying where they had been. It must have been something like the science-fiction stories my family watch on television such as *Startrek*. The body 'dematerialised' as the science-fiction books put it. And that was the end of the continuing existence of the body of Jesus on this earth.

But over a period of six weeks, Jesus 'rematerialised' in all sorts of places – in the garden before Mary of Magdala; on the road to Emmaus behind two sad disciples; in a crowded room behind shut doors; on the shores of Lake Galilee (to cook breakfast for his friends!) ...

Finally he made a very deliberate final disappearance on a hillside outside Jerusalem. This was seen by a crowd of his followers. It seems that Jesus wanted to make it clear that he was leaving them as a body. In the future he was going to come to all of them by means of the Holy Spirit (of which more in the next chapter).

This six-week period when Jesus made repeated 're-materialisations' seems to have had two purposes:

1. To show that Jesus really was alive again.
2. To get the disciples to realise that even though they couldn't see him he might turn up at any moment. It was a sort of game to prepare his followers for the time when they would no longer see him and yet know that he was near.

SO WHAT?

All very interesting you may say but what has it got to do with us? So something remarkable happened centuries ago – what use is it to me, today? Here are three important things that affect all of us.

1. LIFE AFTER DEATH. Listen to what St. Paul thought about it:

> The truth is that Christ has been raised from death, as the guarantee that those who sleep in death will also be be raised.[1]

St. Paul saw the rising of Jesus as we see the first flight of a new design of aircraft. When the first Concorde flew for the first time, the designers didn't say, 'Well, that's the first one off the ground – let's hope we can get the others to do the same!' Of course not. As soon as it flew they knew that all planes *built to the same design* would do the same!

When Jesus rose from the dead to carry on living in an even bigger and greater way it was the proof that all men

1. 1 Cor. 15:20

and women who are, as it were, *built to the same design* will do the same. When the Holy Spirit comes into our lives the likeness is complete and we also shall come back to life after our death.

2. GOOD OVER BAD. In that remarkable fifteenth chapter of 1 Corinthians, St. Paul spells out other important things that are true because of the rising again of Jesus. 'If Christ has not been raised from death,' he said, 'then we have nothing to preach and you have nothing to believe.'[2] When St. Paul first wrote these words in the Greek language he used the word meaning 'empty' to describe the message. Either there is an empty tomb or an empty message, he is saying. What does this mean?

It means that there is no message, no good news, in hearing about a good man who was destroyed by people like us. We live today in a world which has much that is sad and bad. At times we ask ourselves: why try to be good?

But because God raised up Jesus after he had been destroyed and his goodness had been rejected we can see which side is going to win in the end – and the end is *after* death. The very powers of evil 'threw' everything they had at Jesus and at first seemed to win. But God had the last word and it was a good one.

3. FORGIVENESS IS CERTAIN. As we saw in the last chapter the death of Jesus was a deliberate act by God to take the blame for our sins so that he could be seen to be just and yet be able to forgive us. But how do we know that Jesus was the unique, special son of God who could do this for us? The famous hymn says of Jesus:

> There was no other good enough
> To pay the price of sin
> He only could unlock the gate
> Of heaven and let us in.

2. 1 Cor. 15:14

But how do we know Jesus was the one 'good enough to pay the price of sin'? The answer is that we know because God acted to raise him up. 'He was shown with great power,' wrote St. Paul to his friends in Rome, 'to be the Son of God, by being raised from death.'[3]

That is why St. Paul also wrote in 1 Cor. 15:

If Christ has not been raised ... you are still lost in your sins.[4]

But he has – so we are not!

Questions
1. Why is it not possible to say Jesus merely fainted and recovered?
2. What was the odd thing about what was left in the tomb and what does it suggest?
3. Why does it not make sense to say the disciples stole the body and lied?
4. What is the meaning of the resurrection as far as we are concerned?

Passages to Read
1. Luke 24
2. John 20:1–18
3. John 20:24–31 (This shows how the disciples admitted that they found it hard at first to believe that Jesus had risen.)
4. 1 Cor. 15:12–26

3. Rom. 1:4
4. 1 Cor. 15:17

7: His People filled with His Spirit

Exciting though it was for the first Christians to have Jesus back with them after rising from the dead, it was obvious that something big and new was needed. Jesus wanted his followers to make disciples throughout the world. If that was to happen it was going to be difficult if he could only be in one place at one time.

ANOTHER HELPER

Even before his arrest he had been teaching his disciples to expect his replacement by what he described as 'another Helper, the Spirit of truth, to stay with you forever'.[1]

In John's Gospel chapters 14–16 we find much of the teaching about this 'other Helper' and a careful reading of those chapters shows up several important and surprising conclusions.

1. THE ONE GOD IS THREE 'PERSONS'. Look at these words: 'You will not be left all alone; I will come back to you' [14:18]. Jesus is saying that he will be with us when the Holy Spirit comes to us. But a moment later when talking about the obedient Christian he says: 'my Father and I will come to him and live with him' [14:23]. So we are talking about A FATHER, A SON, and A HOLY

1. John 14:16

SPIRIT all at the same time. When people use the term *Holy Trinity*, this is what is meant: the one God is 'tripersonal'.

2. YOU ARE IN TOUCH WITH ALL THREE (OR THE WHOLE OF GOD) WHEN YOU MEET ANY ONE OF THE 'PERSONS'. Jesus wasn't in fact *replaced* by the Holy Spirit. The Spirit made him present with people everywhere. To have the Spirit is to have Jesus. And as we have seen – it is also to have the Father as well [13:23].

3. THE HOLY SPIRIT IS PERSONAL. Look at these words: 'The world cannot receive him, because it cannot see him or know him. But you know him, because he remains with you and is in you' [John 14:17]. Clearly the talk is about a 'he' and not an 'it'.

4. THE HOLY SPIRIT COMES TO THOSE WHO OBEY GOD. 'Whoever loves me will obey my teaching. My Father will love him, and my Father and I will come to him and live with him' [14:23]. This link between our obedience and the coming of the Holy Spirit runs right through the New Testament. That is why 'the world cannot receive him, because it cannot see him or know him' [14:17]. There is evidence in the Bible to show that other people can be *influenced* by the Holy Spirit; but only those who obediently turn to Jesus can *receive* the Spirit. (This is the basic point in the Confirmation service.)

5. THE HOLY SPIRIT IS THE WAY IN WHICH GOD CAN BE IN AND WITH US ALWAYS AND EVERYWHERE. That is why Jesus said: 'It is better for you that I go away, because if I do not go, the Helper will not come to you' [16:17].

ORDERS

When Jesus had made it crystal clear that he was more alive than ever after his crucifixion, he decided to make it equally clear that he was leaving the world. He called his disciples together on a hilltop and before their eyes he was 'taken up into heaven'. The Church calls this moment, the *Ascension*. It marked the end of Jesus working amongst men as a bodily person.

But it also marked the beginning of a new way in which Jesus would work amongst men by the Holy Spirit. Just before he left the disciples he gave clear orders: 'Do not leave Jerusalem, but wait for the gift . . . my Father promised. John baptised with water, but in a few days you will be baptised with the Holy Spirit.'[2]

There was a very important reason for this 'Baptism with the Holy Spirit'. Those first followers were going to be sent out to tell the world about Jesus. Here's how Jesus speaks about it in v.8:

> . . . when the Holy Spirit comes upon you, you will be filled with power, and you will be witnesses for me in Jerusalem, in all Judaea and Samaria, and to the ends of the earth.

The Holy Spirit would bring them the power and abilities to be effective in sharing their news.

So the Apostles obeyed. They waited in Jerusalem, where they had many enemies. And while they waited, they prayed. No doubt they began to get pretty nervous as nothing happened and as Jerusalem filled up with visitors for the Jewish feast of Pentecost.

A STRONG WIND

Then it happened! On the very day of Pentecost itself. Here's how the Book of Acts describes it:

> Suddenly there was a noise from the sky which sounded like a strong wind blowing, and it filled the whole house where they were sitting. Then they saw what looked like tongues of fire which spread out and touched each person

2. Acts 1:4, 5

there. They were all filled with the Holy Spirit and began to talk in other languages, as the Spirit enabled them to speak.[3]

Now all this was very dramatic and there was no doubting about what happened. Once again we see God 'stage-managing' so that the first Christians found *something to hear*, *something to see*, and *something to feel inwardly*. This was very important for them because otherwise they could not have been sure that something really fantastic had happened to them all. Let us note the three particular parts in God's stage-managing.

1. THE SOUND OF A STRONG WIND BLOWING. The Apostles had grown up with the old Hebrew scriptures where the word for the Spirit of God was also the word for 'wind'. The sound made them aware that the Holy Spirit was coming.

2. TONGUES OF FIRE ... AND EACH PERSON ... TOUCHED BY A TONGUE. This brought home to them that each one, leader and follower alike was someone in whom the Holy Spirit could and would work. The noise was general and vague but what they saw was clear and affecting every individual personally. And the fire 'spoke' of burning up the rubbish, therefore of purifying what might be dirty.

3. THEY WERE ALL FILLED WITH THE HOLY SPIRIT AND BEGAN TO TALK IN OTHER LANGUAGES. Those first Christians on the day of Pentecost soon found something exciting happening inside them. They found a feeling of bursting with joy and praise. And when the 'bursting' took place they found they were not praising God in their own language but in others!

Which was rather useful for Jerusalem was packed with foreigners at the time! So God was helping those first Christians to find a great easiness in praising him and also

3. Acts 2:2–4

he was showing them that their praising was meant to be shared by people throughout the world.

So how do we sum up this special event? What does it mean for us today? There are three basic points to remember:

1. THE HOLY SPIRIT IS FOR EACH ONE OF US. The tongues of flame on the day of Pentecost settled on each person separately. In Old Testament times it seems that the Spirit of God came only upon key men and women on special occasions and for special purposes. Now he comes to us all, and that means that *Jesus comes to live in and with us all*.

2. THE HOLY SPIRIT BRINGS NEW POWER INTO OUR LIVES. God is calling Christians to live *above* themselves for him and he promises us the power to live different sorts of lives.

3. THE HOLY SPIRIT CAN CHANGE US FOR THE BETTER. The picture of fire on the day of Pentecost speaks of purifying – of burning up the rubbish and revealing what is good. St. Paul wrote that the 'glory, coming from the Lord, who is the Spirit, transforms us into his likeness, in an ever greater degree of glory.'[4] Very often we are the last to see ourselves changing for the better but if we set put to obey and serve Jesus we open ourselves to this improving work of the Holy Spirit.

A NEW AGE

In the middle of all the excitement and confusion of the day of Pentecost, St. Peter remembered the words of an old Hebrew prophet, Joel. He quoted them to the crowds who gathered around the disciples:

This is what I will do in the last days, God says:
I will pour out my Spirit on everyone;

4. 2 Cor. 3:18

Your sons and your daughters will proclaim my message;
Your young men will see visions,
And your old men will have dreams.[5]

Jeremiah had also prophesied about a new chapter in
God's dealings with men. No longer would it be a case of
people trying to keep the written-down laws of a God they
were told about. 'I will put my law within them and write
it on their hearts; I will be their God and they will be my
people.'[6]

Now with the coming of the Holy Spirit on the day of
Pentecost, the dreams of those old prophets had come true.
A new age had dawned and God was about to bring together
from all over the world and through all the ages: a new
Israel, a new people of God. Becoming a member no longer
depended on being born into a Jewish family. It depended
on being *born again* by the inward working of the Holy
Spirit. Jesus had once said, 'no one can see the Kingdom of
God unless he is born again.'[7]

The crowds that were mobbing St. Peter and his friends
on that day asked what they had to do to join the ranks.
Peter replied: 'Each one of you must turn away from his sins
and be baptised in the name of Jesus Christ, so that your
sins will be forgiven; and you will receive God's gift, the
Holy Spirit.'[8]

Those words apply to you and me today as much as to
those crowds on the day of Pentecost.

A NEW FAMILY

And once we turn away from our sins, and trust Jesus
for our forgiveness and make up our minds to be linked with
him from now on – we also receive the Holy Spirit and are
born again into a new family which the Creed calls the

5. Acts 2:17ff. 6. Jer. 31:33
7. John 3:3 8. Acts 2:38

63

Holy Catholic Church. *Holy* means set apart for God. *Catholic* means extending throughout the world. And *Church* means people who have been called together.

You may feel your local church doesn't quite match up to such a grand description, but it is the local branch of what someone has called 'God's forever family'. And if everyone catches the vision of being a member of the family and plays his part, there's no telling what can happen in any church.

GIFTS

And the part you have to play is more special than you realise because St. Paul taught that the Holy Spirit gives every one of us gifts to use in his service with our fellow Christians. Some may have a remarkable gift (healing is one mentioned) others may have very 'ordinary' gifts ('helping' is another gift mentioned by Paul).[9] The point is that all matter equally to God.

FRUIT

And in our lives, St. Paul taught that the Holy Spirit can plant and bring out the very qualities of character that Jesus shows. As we seek to follow him in daily life we will begin to show the *fruit of the Spirit*, which St. Paul describes as: 'love, joy, peace, patience, kindness, goodness, faithfulness, humility and self-control'.[10]

THE BODY OF CHRIST

No wonder that St. Paul called the Church – *the body of Christ*. If we allow the Holy Spirit to fill us and to produce the very qualities of Jesus in our lives; and if we share the gifts and abilities we have with each other; then Jesus can work through us as a corporate body.

Jesus lives and works in our world today through his

9. 1 Cor 12:1–11
10, Gal 5:22, 23

64

people and by his Spirit. And so it shall be until he returns as a bodily person.

THE LORD'S RETURN

The New Testament Christians believed strongly that one day Jesus would return as a bodily person coming into space and time. They looked forward eagerly to it and hoped it would happen in their time. Jesus said he would return and the Apostles (the leading followers of the time) taught that it was the focus of Christian hope.

This second coming of Jesus will mark the end of the new age of the Spirit. It will be a time when the curtain is rung down on the whole of history and when everyone who has ever lived will stand before the judgment seat of Christ. The dead, we are told, will actually be raised for the event!

But I am happy to say that this solemn time will be a great day of rejoicing for the people of God. Jesus gave this promise to the believer: 'he will not be judged, but has already passed from death to life.'[11]

It is with this great hope ahead of us and strengthened by the Holy Spirit that God's forever family sets about serving Jesus in day-to-day living. Whatever may happen to us, Jesus is with us by his Holy Spirit.

Questions

1. Why was it important for the bodily Jesus to be taken away?
2. Why do we talk about 'the Trinity'?
3. How does the Holy Spirit come to us?
4. What were the lessons that the first Christians were taught by experience on the day of Pentecost?

11. John 5:24

5. What is a Church?
6. What will happen at the end of the 'new age of the Spirit'?

The Creed

Think over the following part of the Apostles' Creed in the light of what you have read:

I believe in the Holy Ghost (Spirit); the holy Catholic Church; the Communion of Saints; the Forgiveness of Sins; the Resurrection of the body; and the life everlasting.

Passages to Read

1. John 14:15–31
2. 1 Cor. 12:1–13
3. 1 Thess. 4:13–18

8: Out of the Old – into the New

I remember hearing a bishop telling how Baptism services used to be held in a part of Africa where he had been working. The scene would be a river. The people who had just become believers would be standing on one bank. They would be dressed in their oldest clothes and walk into the river where the clergyman was waiting. One by one he would gently push them under the water and lift them out as he said, '*I baptise you in the name of the Father, and of the Son and of the Holy Spirit.*'

Then, with big grins and smiles all round, the newly baptised would wade to the other bank, and there they would put on new, fresh clothes. Let us put this into pictures:

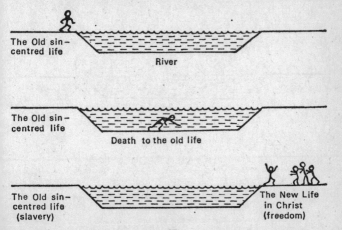

The Old sin-centred life

River

The Old sin-centred life

Death to the old life

The Old sin-centred life (slavery)

The New Life in Christ (freedom)

What the pictures show is that these African Baptism services (which are very like some of the earliest Baptism services in the Church) are a way of making someone act out what God has done for him. God has taken him as someone who was a slave to the life of sin.

He has declared that the person is united with Jesus – the Jesus who died for our sins. So, by going under the water we have a picture of death; of burying the old life.

And by coming out of the water on the other side of the river, we have a picture of being born again, after the death, to a new life in Jesus as a member of God's family circle.

Experts tell us that the picture language of Baptism is a sort of echo of what God did when he led the slave people of the Israelites out of the land of bondage (Egypt) and into the new land as a new nation. So Baptism brings home to us that we too are God's rescued people.

1 The Israelites are blocked by the sea and chased by their old captors

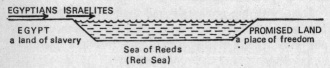

2 The Israelites escape across the sea

Rescue and Life

3 The old captors die as God judges them

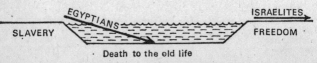

Death to the old life

68

So becoming a Christian is saying goodbye to a life where we are held prisoners by sin; and starting out on a new life as the people of God, with God as our Father, and the Holy Spirit in our lives.

And if we say that Jesus was dying for us then we are saying that you and I were actually *there* on the cross with and in him! And that means that when Jesus rose again to new life then you and I were *there* with him and in him also. It's a difficult idea but it's an exciting one!

And when we go 'under the water of Baptism' that is a picture of going down to death with Jesus. And when we come 'up' again – that is a picture of rising to a new life with him. Here's how St. Paul put it:

> By our baptism, then, we were buried with him and shared his death, in order that, just as Christ was raised from death by the glorious power of the Father, so also we might live a new life.[1]

So because of being linked to Jesus we are rescued from the old life of being trapped in sin and are set free to live a new life – not just after death but here and now.

But, of course, *this must be something that we want*. So in our Baptism *we* are saying and doing something.

MY PART

When I am baptised:

1. I am turning away from living a sin-centred life. This is what the word *REPENTING* means.
2. I am trusting that my sinful self has been put to death with Jesus. This is what *BELIEVING* means.
3. I am wanting to set out on a new life as a member of God's family, helped by the Holy Spirit and following the way of Jesus. This is where *OBEYING* comes in.

Notice those three words:

1. Rom. 6:4

REPENTING
BELIEVING
OBEYING

HEY – WAIT A MINUTE!

'But,' some of you may say, 'I've already been baptised when I was a baby and somewhere in the house there's a certificate to prove it!'

Good. And let me point out that when you were baptised, your parents and godparents made those Baptism promises for you because they felt they had the right to speak on your behalf. They promised that you would repent, believe and obey.

But now things are different. You are old enough to make your own mind up about these things. As a baby the water of Baptism was poured over your head because of the promises other people made for you. You were declared to be a Christian because of those promises.

But now what about it? Nobody makes your promises for you now! Do you want to change your mind about all this? God doesn't hold prisoners – he wants us to be free to be what we really want to be.

CONFIRMATION

So here is where we face up to what the Confirmation service is all about. It is a chance for us to say 'Yes' to those promises other people made for us when we were babies.

YES – TO REPENTING
YES – TO BELIEVING
YES – TO OBEYING

You have got to decide whether you really want to be a Christian and if you go forward at the Confirmation service you are telling the whole wide world – YES!

Yes – I do want to turn my back on living for anything and anyone other than Jesus Christ. *Yes* – I do believe that

70

he has died for me and that he has taken me with him through death and judgment for my sins. And *yes* – I will (with God's help) obey and follow Jesus for the rest of my life.

WHY WAIT?

But if this is how you feel, why wait until the Confirmation service? Perhaps you have already said 'the big *YES*'. If so then you know that you are a Christian *now* in every sense of the word.

1. You are forgiven.
2. You are a child of God.
3. You have the gift of the Holy Spirit in you and with you.

And don't take my word for it – listen to the words of the Bible:

1. YOU ARE FORGIVEN

He will forgive us our sins and purify us from all our wrongdoing.[2]

2. YOU ARE A CHILD OF GOD

It is through faith that all of you are God's sons in union with Christ Jesus.[3]

3. YOU HAVE THE GIFT OF THE HOLY SPIRIT IN YOU AND WITH YOU.

To show that you are his sons, God sent the Spirit of his Son into our hearts . . .[4]

SEAL IT WITH A PRAYER

Let me suggest a prayer that will make what your Baptism talks about become real for you from this moment on. Read the words. Think about them. And then, if you are quite sure you want to, pray this prayer where you are and mean it.

2. 1 John 1:9   3. Gal. 3:26   4. Gal. 4:6

Dear Heavenly Father
Thank you for making me and loving me.
Thank you for all that Baptism talks
about –
for the fact that Jesus died for my sins
and for the fact that I can share
in rising with him to a new life.
I want that to be true for me.
I turn from my sinfulness and I
trust in what Jesus has done for me.
Please come into my life by your
Holy Spirit and help me to obey
you in all the days ahead.
For Jesus's sake. Amen.

No one who sincerely prays a prayer like that will stay the same. And those who come to God in this sort of way can be sure that God will come into their lives.

Come near to God, and he will come near to you.[5]

Questions
1. What is being acted out in our Baptism?
2. What is the Baptism service saying about God's promise to us?
3. What is the Baptism service saying about *our* promise to God?

Passages to Read
1. Acts 2:37–42
2. Acts 16:16–34
3. Matt. 28:16–20

5. Jas. 4:8

72

9: Living the New Life

'No – no! You've got it all wrong,' cried Sue, who was getting fed up with Harry's know-all way of speaking. 'Christianity is not about you and me being good. It's about Jesus saving us by dying for us. And all we have to do is, just believe!'

'Rubbish, Sue,' replied Harry, in just the sort of pompous way she couldn't stand. 'Just believing gets us nowhere. My vicar says Christianity is about living the way Jesus wants us to live.'

'Well your vicar's wrong – that's all,' snapped Susan. 'Our Bible class leader was only talking about this last Sunday. And he kept quoting a verse from – er – Ephesians, I think it was.'

'And what did that say – *if* you can remember?'

'Of course I can remember. Just stop talking and give me a moment! Ah yes – something about being saved by grace so that we've nothing to boast about. That's right! Being saved by God's grace and not our works. So that proves it. We don't have to do anything. So you were wrong – see?'

* * *

As a matter of fact Harry and Susan were both wrong. And – in a way – they were both right as well! The trouble was that they couldn't see that they were talking about two different things.

Susan was talking about *becoming* a Christian. And she was right. There's no good thing we can do that will *earn* our forgiveness.

But Harry was talking about *being* a Christian after you have become one. And he was right. We are called to live new lives for Jesus.

STAND BY FOR A CHILDREN'S STORY!

Let me tell a children's story! Once upon a time there was a large house with a large garden and it was owned by a grubby old man who never looked after it.

All the children in the area soon learned that they could walk into the house and run around in the garden whenever they liked. The grubby old man didn't seem to mind what they did. He never tried to stop the children doing anything they wanted. If they wanted to dig holes – he let them. If they wanted to tear up the carpets – he didn't stop them. If they wanted to leave rubbish everywhere – it seemed that he couldn't care less.

As a result what seemed such a wonderful place became more and more of a smelly mess, and because everybody tried to do exactly what he or she wanted the house and garden became a place of selfishness and unhappiness. Plus more and more rubbish!

One day a stranger came to the house and looked around at all that he could see. He saw that the house and garden was a wonderful place for the children to play in, but he also saw that the children were destroying the house, the garden and even their own happiness. He thought this was very sad.

The stranger went away and thought about it. Then he made up his mind. He sold his house, his car, and all his furniture. He drew out all his savings and he went to the grubby old man at the house and garden and bought it. The old man went away quite happily. He didn't really care for the house, or the garden, and certainly not for the children.

Then the stranger asked all the children in the neighbourhood to come and meet him in the garden. When they all had come together he stood up and spoke to them.

'Children,' he said, 'the only thing I want is for you all to be happy. When I saw how you were all becoming so unhappy I went away and sold everything I had so that I could buy this house, just for you.

'The grubby old man who owned the house has gone and now I am in charge. Everything is different now and we can start all over again.

'But if you are going to be happy then you must stop playing here in the way you used to. All that did was destroy the place, and it kept you fighting each other because everyone wanted his own way.

'I have set you free to start again here. But if you want to stay with me then you must play in a different way. You must look after each other and look after the house and the garden. I have given everything I owned to set you free from the old ways. Now I ask you to give everything you have to make this a place of happiness for everyone.

'And if you do, then I will help you in every way I can!'

SIX POINTS TO NOTE

The story makes the following points:
1. The children didn't pay a penny towards the cost of the house and garden. They could never have raised between them anything like the cost.
2. The stranger by sacrificing all he owned bought the house.
3. There was now a new start and all the children were welcome to come.
4. But because everything was new, there had to be a new

way of behaving. If this hadn't been the case, everything would slip back to the old unhappy mess again.

5. The example for the new way of behaving was the unselfishness of the stranger. He called the children to imitate him.

6. The stranger promised to help all those children who tried to follow his example.

BECOMING A CHRISTIAN AND BEING A CHRISTIAN

There are no prizes for those who guess the reason why I told this children's story! It is a picture of what Jesus has done for us and what we must do for him. Let me spell out what I mean:

1. We can become Christians only because of the wonderful, unselfish love of God which we see in Jesus. So Sue and her Bible class leader were both right. We cannot add anything to the price Jesus paid. What is needed here from us is BELIEVING.

2. *But to be a Christian* means we must *want* no part of the selfish and sinful life that we used to be involved in. This is what REPENTING means.

3. And the Christian not only turns away *from* the old life and its way of behaving, he turns *to* the new life and sets out to live it. This involves OBEYING.

4. The example to copy is the example of the totally unselfish Jesus. St. Paul once said, 'Imitate me, then, just as I imitate Christ.'[1] So obeying means IMITATING. And this is where Harry and his vicar were right.

5. And God promises to help those who set out to live like this. The way he does this is through the power and presence of the Holy Spirit. In Acts 5:32 we read that the Holy Spirit 'is God's gift to those who obey him'.

1. 1 Cor. 11:1

COPING WITH OUR FAILURES

So the Christian is called upon to live in a new way because God has given him a new life. We must look at what this new way of living involves but before we do there is something we must be very clear about. And here it is – *we Christians will always be sinners*. What we are going to think about must never become a set of rules that have to be kept if we are to remain Christians.

A church is a place for sinners only. God knows the temptations and pressures we are under and he is always ready to forgive when we admit to our needs and failures. Jesus said that the people who really belong to God's Kingdom are those who realise how poor they are spiritually.[2]

Let me give you an illustration I find helpful. In the Christian life you and I are like children trying to learn to walk. Now if you've ever seen a toddler taking his first steps you will know they are full of accidents and sudden flops! But we all chuckle! The bottom area is usually well padded and we're all around to pick the child up.

But supposing the house was on fire, and the child's very life depended on being able to walk out, and we were outside unable to help. That would be a terrible situation.

Now we are children learning to walk the new life with Jesus – and there is no fire. We are safe even when we fall over. And we shall fall down – many times. And we shall never come to a point when we couldn't be better Christians.

Remember this as you read through the next page or so.

NEW LIVES FOR OLD

In the last chapter we read how in some parts of Africa those who get baptised act out the putting off of their old life and then the putting on of a new life.

2. Matt. 5:3

This is the sort of thing St. Paul had in mind when he wrote the third chapter of his letter to the Colossians. In that chapter we can see that he tells his readers that there are certain things they must:

        a) 'put to death' v.5
        b) 'get rid of'   v.8
        c) 'take off'   v.9

And the things he lists as such are such things as:

immorality	greed	insults
indecency	anger	obscene talk
lust	hateful feelings	
evil passions		

We may feel that these are not the sort of things that we see in our lives. But the world we live in is full of these things and it is almost impossible for us not to be affected. Further, a really honest look at ourselves will show that we share the same sinful nature as anyone else. So we are called to see those sinful things and to shun them.

But to leave it with a list of things we shouldn't do isn't very helpful, and St. Paul doesn't. He is thinking of the of taking off old clothes and putting on new ones and he knew the best way to get rid of bad qualities is to crowd them out with better ones. So here are the sorts of 'clothes' to put on:

compassion	gentleness	being forgiving
kindness	patience	plus: lots of love!
humility	tolerance	

TRY ON THE CLOTHES

If you are like me, you may well by now be thinking that all this is beyond you! These qualities are just too much like Jesus, and you and I are nowhere near so good!

Perhaps some readers may even feel like giving up. Here therefore are a few things to remember:

1. God loves us.
2. God knows our limitations.
3. We are safe in his love even when we go wrong.
4. God can pick us up again, when we fall down.

WE PUT ON AND GOD PUTS IN

But there is something even more comforting to know. This is that the qualities of life that we are being called to 'put on' are the very qualities that the Holy Spirit of God can put *in*. Look at these words also from St. Paul:

The Spirit produces love, joy, peace, patience, kindness, goodness, faithfulness, humility and self control.[3]

It's an almost identical list of qualities to the one we were looking at earlier! *GOD PUTS IN WHAT WE TRY TO PUT ON!*

NOT ALL AT ONCE

But let me share a couple of other things I've learned. The first is that everything doesn't change at once. After all a newly wed couple often have quite a time adjusting to the job of living with and for each other. It's just the same in the matter of living with and for Jesus.

The second point is that we are usually the least qualified to know how much progress we are making. I would get worried if someone told me how well he was doing at being a Christian!

THE BIG LIE

One of the sad facts of life is that the Devil has done a pretty good job in spreading around *the big lie* about life. We are surrounded by people who have been fooled into believing that a life of kindness, patience, forgiveness, love, unselfishness and so on is boring and dull.

3. Gal. 5:22, 23

The exciting way to live – many say – is to do what you want to do and be free of rules and examples to follow. We Christians need to see this as *the big lie*. The truth is exactly the other way around. Jesus's way of life is the happiest and best.

Questions

1. What does it mean to say 'we are saved by grace and not by good deeds'?
2. What are the 'clothes' we most need to wear at school, at home, on the sports field?
3. What do we have to do if the Holy Spirit is to put in his fruit?
4. Why is there no need to feel depressed if we fall short of the example of Jesus?

Passages to Read

1. Gal. 5:13–24
2. 1 Pet. 2:9–12
3. Matt. 5:1–14

10: The Family Together

'You know,' says the little man who's just been rescued from the crooked sheriff, 'I never asked his name!'

He's talking to a friend and they are both looking at a masked (but oh so very good!) cowboy who is riding away with his Red-Indian helper. The masked cowboy had personally rescued the little man from being thrown out of his own farmhouse and run out of town.

The friend turns with a look of surprise. 'Don't you know?' he says. 'That's the Lone Ranger!'

And so ends yet another television episode of the masked cowboy hero (not forgetting Tonto the Indian and, of course, Silver, the horse!) It's a pretty old T.V. series but, like *Batman*, it keeps coming back!

NOT LONELY HEROES

There's always something attractive about lonely heroes. Many books are written about such people. But there's something we must get clear right now about ourselves as Christians.

We are not meant to be lonely heroes. God's plan is for us to be born again into new families. And those families are the churches to which we belong. Of course there are times – sometimes quite long periods – when we will find ourselves without much in the way of fellowship, but those are not meant to be what God intends for us normally.

In later chapters in this book we shall be thinking about our personal prayers and our personal Bible reading, but nothing is more important than properly belonging to a church where the people see themselves as members of God's family.

St. Peter once suggested that the individual Christian was like a 'living stone'. But notice what he said:

> Come as living stones, and let yourselves be used in building the spiritual temple.[1]

The point he is making is that God can do a lot more when he puts us together, than he can if he were to leave us lying around the place. A pile of bricks is pretty useless until builders come with their skills and make a house out of them. God wants to do some building and we are all living stones that he wants to put together with other living stones.

LET'S STOP AND SEE WHAT WE HAVE LEARNED:
1.   Christians are not meant to be 'loners'.
2.   God can do more with Christians when he brings them together into churches.
3.   Churches are meant to be families.

WHAT DOES GOD WANT HIS FAMILIES TO DO?

God wants us to live in families so that:
1.   We can worship him better.
2.   We can learn from him better.
3.   We can encourage each other.
4.   We can serve him better in the world.
    Let us look at these four things.

1. 1 Pet. 2:4

1. WORSHIPPING

Now with any other sort of family we would think that the father was pretty 'big-headed' if he said that he wanted his children to worship him. But we are talking about Almighty God. And giving God our worship and praise is right, and it does something good to us also.

As a matter of fact saying nice things about others always does something good for you! The people 'who never have a good word to say about anyone' are never, never nice to know. And few things, if any, are more refreshing than joining with others and totally forgetting oneself in giving praise and adoration to the one who made us and our world, and who came in Jesus to show how much he cares for us.

Someone has said: 'Heaven comes down when our praises go up'. A time of worship is a time when we learn to put first things first. We put God above all the things that have been on the top of our minds and we remind ourselves of his greatness and love. And that helps to get our worries into their proper place.

And worship is a time of thanking God. It is a time of celebrating all the good things the Lord has done for us. I know of one church where many of the women put on long dresses for church – because that is what they would do if they were celebrating anything else.

Perhaps someone reading these words may be saying, 'That's all very well but sometimes I find myself in a pretty empty and unfriendly church and I feel I get nothing out of it'. I know such churches exist. But worship is not about 'what you get out of it': it is about what you put in. You do indeed get blessing and help from God *out* of worship but *the amount you get out is related to the amount you put in*.

So you may not like the hymn tunes, and the organist may have cloth fingers, and the vicar may be having an off day – but that needn't stop you offering God your thanks and praise as best you can. And worship, of course, includes praying and bringing our problems, fears, wishes and hopes to God. And not only our personal matters, but also joining with the rest of the congregation to pray together for other things.

2. LEARNING

The place where the church meets is not only our family gathering place, it is also our school. In every service the Bible should be read and through the sermon or talk we should be helped to see how Almighty God is to be understood and served in day-to-day living.

And there are other ways of learning besides listening. We learn from each other when we discuss our beliefs and experiences together. Most churches these days have groups where discussion and Bible study takes place.

Once again I can hear some reader saying that in his or her church the sermons are pretty poor and so on. My answer would be this: try hard to find something helpful in every talk or sermon. Even the worst sermons usually have something valuable in them. And if there are things you couldn't understand – ask the preacher afterwards.

You can say I told you to!

3. ENCOURAGING

I said earlier that we weren't meant to be 'Lone Rangers' but nevertheless we can't take our church with us to work or school or wherever we may be having to go. There are large parts of our time when we have to be alone.

Because of this, coming together for worship on Sunday can be a very encouraging time as we meet again with the others in the family. In the Letter to the Hebrews we read: 'Let us not give up the habit of meeting together, as some are doing. Instead, let us encourage one another . . .'[2]

2. Heb. 10:25

And it's good if people of all ages are in church together. It reminds us that we are a real family. The young church member may be wondering whether his faith will stand the test of time. A glance across the church at older members is encouraging. And some of those older members get a great deal of encouragement when they see youngsters worshipping with them.

We all need each other!

4. SERVING

If becoming a Christian is joining God's family circle (and it is) then we have to realise that God is running a family business! And you know what family businesses are like; everyone in the family is involved.

Jesus said to his first followers, 'As the Father sent me, so I send you.'[3] Every church is meant to be a 'Godsend' to its neighbourhood. We Christians are meant to provide the evidence to others that God is a loving Father. He wants to meet the needs of everyone.

A man's greatest need is to find Jesus as his own rescuer and leader in life. This is good news that we must all share both amongst our friends and also as churches within our neighbourhoods. But people have many other needs. That is why many churches run all kinds of activities in a neighbourhood. And that is why Christians can find themselves working for more fairness in society by taking part in local and national politics and movements.

But all that we do ourselves or as churches is meant to come out of loving our Father and loving our neighbour as ourselves. If we love God then we don't want to see him ignored by those around us or to see his standards for living forgotten.

And if we love our neighbours then we cannot want to

3. John 20:21

see them missing out on all that God can give them, nor can we ignore those who are suffering from injustice, poverty, or sickness.

A final word here – your church is meant to be the place where love for God and love for each other meet. Jesus was very clear about this when he spoke to the first Christians:

> And now I give you a new commandment: love one another. As I have loved you, so you must love one another. If you have love for one another, then everyone will know that you are my disciples.[4]

THE BODY OF CHRIST

St. Paul, as we saw earlier, taught that Christians, working together, were the 'body of Christ'. The Holy Spirit has given us gifts of one sort and another, and if we use those gifts in serving him together then the work of Jesus will continue where we are.

> Under his control all the different parts of the body fit together, and the whole body is held together by every joint with which it is provided. So when each separate part works as it should, the whole body grows and builds itself up through love.[5]

Your church is meant to be the body of Christ in your area. But Christ's body will be deformed and crippled unless everyone is playing their part and using their gifts.

THE SERVICE THAT SAYS IT ALL

The Lord's Supper or Holy Communion service is the service that says it all for the Christian.

4. John 13:34
5. Eph. 4:16

- *It tells us what God has done for us (in the death of Jesus for us).*
- *It tells us what God is doing for us (in bringing us together as families).*
- *It tells us what God will do for us (it is a picture of the great party awaiting us in heaven).*

The Lord's Supper is like Baptism because it makes us act out something that is true and very important. In Baptism we saw that we acted out dying to the old life and being born again to the new life with Jesus. In the Communion service we act out the truth that Jesus has died for each one of us and so made it possible for us to be in the Father's family.

(There is a special name for this sort of service where the message is put across by making people act it out. It's called a *sacrament*).

Here's what we act out in the Holy Communion service.

1. JESUS DIED FOR US. This is the central fact of the service and nothing must get in the way of us seeing it. The bread and wine are given a special meaning at the service.

> ... every time you eat of this bread and drink from this cup you proclaim the Lord's death until he comes.[6]

Behind all the food we eat there is always a story. There is the death of animals and vegetables. There is the work of many hands at many stages – sowing, harvesting, processing, cooking. There's a price behind everything we eat. And the price is often death so that we might live. But when Jesus said those words over the bread and the wine he was making something clear to us all. What brings us together as people who can be accepted into the family of a holy God, is his broken body and shed blood.

6. 1 Cor. 11:26

But now, by means of the physical death of his Son, God has made you his friends.[7]

And just as we draw normal life from normal food, so we draw eternal life from what the bread and wine 'talk' about: *the death of Jesus for us*.

2. WE ARE A FAMILY. The people of the Church are united around what is often called the *Lord's Table*. We share bread and wine from that table. We are reminded that God has made us a family and is wanting us to love one another. In some churches, before everyone gathers around the table there is a moment called 'The Peace' where everyone greets one another. This brings home to us that God wants us to belong to each other.

3. WE ARE FORGIVEN SINNERS. But the service does not stop when the bread and wine are put on the table and the words are spoken which give them the special meaning.

We are there to eat and drink.

The death of Jesus for us will not help us and take away the blame for our sins unless we say 'yes' to it. And we swallow far more than bread and wine in that service. *We swallow our pride*. As we eat and drink each one of us is saying, 'Yes, I am a sinner and I continually need the forgiveness that is mine because Jesus died for my sins on the cross.'

4. WE ARE BEING NOURISHED BY CHRIST. Again, just as food at the meal tables gives us the energy to keep going, so what the Communion service shows is that Jesus will nourish us in our new lives for him, if we keep in touch with him and his family. And because we are doing just this in the service, we are nourished through the service. The bread and wine speak mainly about the death of Jesus for us. But as we eat and drink we can think over St. Paul's words: 'He gave us his son – will he not also freely give us all

7. Col. 1:22

things?'[8] *To take part in this service thoughtfully will nourish and strengthen us as spiritual people. We may be feeding on bread but we are inwardly also feeding on Christ.*

5. WE ARE GOING TO HEAVEN! There is a sense in which the Communion service is like a T.V. action replay in reverse. The replay is taking place *before* the action! If you can make head or tail of that!

Jesus used to picture heaven as a great banquet. Those who have been forgiven are the guests and the party is never over.

Until that time the Communion service gives us a little reminder of the glories of heaven to come when all God's children through the ages will be gathered together to enjoy a life free from sin, suffering and all that isn't good and lovely.

St. Matthew records that when Jesus conducted the first-ever Lord's Supper, within hours of being sent to die, he said these words as his disciples drank:

I tell you, I will never again drink this wine until the day I drink the new wine with you in my Father's Kingdom.[9]

Questions
1. Why does God plan for Christians to belong in 'families'?
2. How can younger Christians encourage older Christians?
3. What is the main meaning of the Holy Communion service?
4. How can I worship God in a poorly attended church where the service seems to be dull?

8. Rom. 8:32
9. Matt. 26:29

5. *Who* is the local church meant to be serving?
6. How can Christ's body be deformed today?

Passages to Read
1. Rom. 12:1–8
2. Eph. 3:7–10
3. 1 Cor. 11:23–26

11: Out in the Big Wide World

'Funny people, that lot in number fourteen!'

'Oh you mean the Browns? Yes – they are, aren't they?'

'Keep themselves to themselves all the time. You never see them around do you? Mind you, they seem to have a happy time in there. I'd like to be a fly on the wall. Lots of singing and laughter. But they never have so much as a "good morning" for the rest of us!'

'Oh – I wouldn't say that. I've often seen them smile at me when we pass in the street. But it never goes any further. Strange, isn't it?'

'Strange isn't the word I'd use. Unfriendly, I call it!'

* * *

There's something very odd about a family that hardly ventures outside its front door. And for all I've been saying about the importance of Christians properly belonging to their churches we shall probably spend more time away from our new 'families' than actually with them.

Our heavenly Father wants his families and his children to be *outgoing* and not to keep themselves to themselves. But if we are going to spend most of our lives 'out there' amongst people who mostly don't see God as we see him then there are going to be pressures that affect us.

So – be prepared! Or as St. Peter put it:

Have your minds ready for action... Be obedient to God, and do not allow your lives to be shaped by those desires that you had when you were still ignorant.[1]

THE WORLD

The Bible speaks about the world in different ways. It says that God made the world and yet in other places we are told not to love the world. Why is this?

The answer is to be found in this parable of Jesus:

Jesus told them another parable: 'The Kingdom of heaven is like this. A man sowed good seed in his field. One night, when everyone was asleep, an enemy came and sowed weeds among the wheat and went away. When the plants grew and the ears of corn began to form, then the weeds showed up. The man's servants came to him and said, "Sir, it was good seed you sowed in your field; where did the weeds come from?" "It was some enemy who did this," he answered. "Do you want us to go and pull up the weeds?" they asked him. "No," he answered, "because as you gather the weeds you might pull up some of the wheat along with them. Let the wheat and the weeds both grow together until the harvest. Then I will tell the harvest workers to pull up the weeds first, tie them in bundles and burn them, and then to gather in the wheat and put it in my barn." '[2]

The field in the parable was the world, and it was indeed made by God. He 'sowed' plenty of goodness into it. But, as Jesus put it: there is an Enemy. The Bible writers were very clear about the existence of this Enemy. And because the human race through the centuries has chosen selfish ways rather than God-centred ways – the influence of the Enemy is huge.

1. 1 Pet. 1:13, 14
2. Matt. 13:24–30

So we have a good world, designed to be the place for us to live in and enjoy; but badly spoiled. Indeed St. John described the Enemy or the Devil, as 'The Ruler of this world'.[3]

However we know from Jesus's story that the Enemy's power is limited. God will have the last word and those who put their trust in Christ are 'rescued ... from the power of darkness and brought ... safe into the Kingdom of his dear Son, by whom we are set free, that is, our sins are forgiven.'[4]

LIVING IN BETWEEN

We live in between the creation of a good world and the final harvest which will destroy all the Enemy's influence. And during this period Jesus has a special job for Christians to be doing:

> You are like light for the whole world ... your light must shine before people, so that they will see the good things you do and praise your Father in heaven.[5]

Now light – as Jesus said at the time – is no use unless it is brought into the dark areas. That's what it's for. So if we are to do what Jesus expects us to do – we have got to spend a great deal of our time out in the darkness of the Enemy-controlled world.

Which is exactly what Jesus did when he came into the world to live and die for us. 'God loved the world so much that he gave his only Son ...' wrote St. John.[6] We ourselves are meant to go out into the world from our church 'families' and make God's love known.

Before we go any further – let me sum up what I have been saying about the world.

3. John 14:30   4. Col. 1:13, 14
5. Matt. 5:14–16   6. John 3:16

1. The world was made by God for his children.
2. The world has been spoiled by the work of the Enemy.
3. The Enemy is now public influence number one.
4. The world is still loved by God.
5. The world is meant to *see* a loving God in the good things we do.
6. The world will be judged and put right by God.

UNDER PRESSURE

Now if you and I are going to spend a great deal of our time in a spoiled world then we are going to be in a certain amount of danger. The danger is that of getting overwhelmed.

It's rather like a boat and water. A boat is made to sail on water just as we were made to live in the world. But if you watch an expert sailor in a racing dingy you will see that he takes a great deal of care to keep the boat balanced and trimmed. If he ships in too much of what he's sailing on, he will end up waterlogged or capsized and going nowhere!

So Christians are under many pressures which could submerge them if they are not continually awake to the dangers. And all the pressures have one thing in common – they are pressures to conform to what 'everyone else' is doing. St. Paul warned us: 'Do not conform yourselves to the standards of this world.'[7]

I want to mention three particular pressures which will threaten all young Christians really wanting to let their light shine before men.

1. POSSESSIONS

There's no doubt about it, we live in an age which worships possessions. Just walk around any shopping area and you can see tempting displays in the shops of clothes,

7. Rom. 12:2

shoes, cameras, radios, records, hi-fi, motor bikes, cars, labour-saving gadgets and more.

First of all let's be clear about this. It is not wrong to have possessions and we need food and clothes and so on. Nor should we go to the extremes of saying all luxuries are wrong.

What *is* wrong is when we find ourselves 'hooked' on possessions: wanting this thing, then that thing, then this thing and so on. Money and what we can buy can become a god who gets our daily worship! Jesus saw this danger years ago and said pretty bluntly:

No one can be a slave of two masters; he will hate one and love the other; he will be loyal to one and despise the other. You cannot serve both God and money.[8]

Let me suggest a few questions to ask about anything we want to possess:
1. Do I need it?
2. Will it enrich my life?
3. Is it something I can share with others?

Let's think them through. Obviously if we need something, then there's no argument. Jesus taught us to ask God for our 'daily bread' – which means our real needs. But let's consider the other two questions.

WILL IT ENRICH MY LIFE? If one is a music lover then I believe a record collection and a decent record player can be something enriching. But if you just love playing with gadgets (and many of us do!) then I would want to ask whether buying expensive hi-fi equipment would be right. I've noticed that these things tend to come in and out of fashion. Once we all lived happily without cassette recorders. Then we all 'have' to have them. Then what we need are stereo-cassette recorders – and so it goes on.

IS IT SOMETHING I CAN SHARE WITH OTHERS? Look at

8. Matt. 6:24

this third question. I know of a wonderful Christian couple who are pretty wealthy and bought themselves a big house. Now I could have said that they didn't need such a big house, but I saw what they did with it. They opened it for church meetings, for people to come and rest and so on. They saw their possessions as something God gave them to share.

And that is the right use of possessions.

2. SEX

Another very obvious pressure today upon us all is the pressure of sex.

Now it is important to see that sex is God's idea and therefore a very good one! God wants men and women to find fun and fulfilment in sexual relationships.

But the danger with an over-emphasis on sex is that we look on girls, or boys, as objects from which we can get fun and pleasure. That is to start thinking of people as *things* which is to forget that God made men and women in his own image.

Again something that is good can be harmful if it is not used in the proper way. I remember a friend of mine swinging a cricket bat into my ear! I was right behind him and he didn't think carefully before he practised a big hit. As a result I was the one that got hit, and hurt!

In the same way sexual intercourse between a man and a woman can be wrong and harmful. It is far more than enjoying each other. It does something within our minds and personalities. You are never the same again afterwards with regard to each other. God meant it to be the purple passage within a relationship that goes on and on. To make love without careful thought, deep respect and the intention of staying together is to miss the best and is likely to cause inner hurt. The Bible is pretty blunt – it says it is sinful.

In other words – sex is for marriage. The physical act of

96

love is a way of saying, 'absolutely everything that is me belongs to you!' To try to 'say' that to several people is to become a liar.

'But,' say lots of people, 'that's old-fashioned. Everybody does it now.' And when you hear people say this (often well-known people writing in the newspapers) you begin to feel an old 'square' and ashamed to admit if you have no sexual experience yourself.

The truth is usually this – many young people like to give the impression of being sexually adventurous. As often as not they are bluffing because they too have been kidded into believing that the 'big' thing to do is to have had sexual experience. So stick to your guns and don't be fooled! If a boy at work or school says to you, 'I've had sex with several girls,' what he is really saying is this: 'I have acted with several girls as if I totally belonged to each one of them and to no one else.' In other words: *'I've cheated each one of them.'*

But sometimes what happens is that a young couple who are very fond of each other find that 'they got carried away'. I want to say two things.

Firstly if this really did happen, don't for a moment think God cannot forgive and forget what they have done. Of course he can; and will, if they are sorry.

Secondly, the reason why it happened was probably because the young couple were spending far *too much time alone by themselves*. It is far wiser to go around with your friends most of the time and when you go out together by yourselves be sensible about not walking into temptation.

A lot of serious-minded young Christians get over anxious because of having 'sinful' thoughts or dreams about sexual matters. It is important to remember that our sexual instincts are given us by God and reactions to seeing some lurid book cover or film poster are not necessary sinful at all. It's when we *dwell* on such thoughts that it becomes wrong. That's when we start thinking of the opposite sex as *things* and not *people*.

And God knows only too well how often we are bombarded with pictures, photographs, books, words, dirty jokes and so on every day. *He* knows the unfair pressures that are put on us.

The best way to be pure-minded is to concentrate on putting *in* good things rather than on trying to push *out* bad things. Try to fill your mind with what is good; as St. Paul said:

> In conclusion, my brothers, fill your minds with those things that are good, and that deserve praise: things that are true, noble, right, pure, lovely, and honourable.[9]

To sum up here are a few guidelines:

1. Sex is God's idea and therefore it is good.
2. Sex, like all good things, can be spoiled and misused.
3. Don't be selfish with your girlfriend or boyfriend. Put the other person's best interests first.
4. Don't spend too much time alone with your girlfriend or boyfriend. Share yourselves with others – you will all enjoy this.
5. It is natural from time to time to have sexual thoughts and feelings. What is wrong is to dwell on them.
6. God knows about the pressures we are under and does not blame us for those.

3. POPULARITY

Deep within us we all like to be popular. There's nothing wrong about that.

But this desire to be popular has another side to it, *which is that we don't like to be unpopular!* And this is where things can go wrong.

Nobody likes to 'stick out like a sore thumb' and so when

9. Phil. 4:8

we are in the company of those who are not yet Christians there is a *pressure on us to conform* – to be exactly the same as everybody else. As we saw earlier in this chapter, Paul warned us not to 'conform ... to the standards of this world'.[10]

But not conforming can be very difficult. Sometimes a Christian can find himself in a position where *everyone* is doing something that is not strictly right. It could be in class or at work. You may be told at work to cover up for someone else who has slipped off early. If you tell the truth it's the *other* person who gets into trouble. So *you* won't be very popular!

Not easy is it? But we have to make it clear to the others that while we don't want to get them into trouble – we are under orders to be honest. It's often amazing to see how people respect us for this. But not always!

Then there is the *pressure to deny*. When Jesus was taken off to be put on trial for his life, Peter plucked up the courage to follow him and to sit around in the courtyard near where the trial was taking place.

However when people surrounded him and tried to make him admit to being a follower of Jesus, he couldn't stand up to the pressure. 'I do not know the man you are talking about!' was his answer.[11] And before we run him down we must admit that it is very easy to deny Jesus even without saying the sorts of things that Peter said.

Don't be afraid to stick up for Jesus! You will find the greatest friend in the world is helping you at such a time!

Behind all our longings to be popular is this feeling inside of wanting to be loved. The thing that we must never forget is that whatever anyone else may feel about us – our heavenly Father loves us more deeply than we will ever understand.

10. Rom. 12:2
11. Mark 14:71

God has shown us how much he loves us – it was while we were still sinners that Christ died for us ... We were God's enemies, but he made us his friends through the death of his Son.[12]

So whenever you feel that everyone is against you, just remember that the most important person of all thinks you are rather special! Praise the Lord!

Questions

1. What is the proper Christian way of looking at the world around him?
2. What is the main pressure that 'the world' puts on the Christian?
3. We have thought of three types of pressure on young Christians. What others can you think of?
4. What is the best way to try to keep out impure thoughts?
5. Why does God want his children to go out into the world?
6. What actions are Christians (and should Christians) be taking to make the world a better place?

Passages to Read

1. Gen. 2:18–25 (The purpose of sex and marriage.)
2. Deut. 8:11–20 (Wealth and faithfulness to God.)
3. 2 Tim. 4:10

12. Rom. 5:8, 10

12: The Ever-Open Line

'So if you would like to put your question to the Prime Minister the lines are now open . . .'

The 'phone-in' radio or television programme is now a regular feature and it has become a way in which totally unknown people can find themselves talking to some of the most important people of the day.

But the exciting thing I want to share with you is that you and I can call up the ruler of the universe at all times. The line is always open.

In other words, we are talking about prayer.

DIFFICULTIES

People often tell me that they find praying diificult. Certainly I would have to say that my prayer life has a long way to go, so I sympathise. But I can't say I find praying itself to be difficult.

I think the difficulties we have at first in praying can usually be traced to two false ideas:

1. *That there is a special language which is needed before one can pray properly.*
2. *That there are some things you cannot pray about.*

Now we must see these ideas as absolutely wrong. The big thing about praying is to remember who you are talking to. And Jesus put it simply when he said: 'pray to your

Father, who is unseen'.[1] It is our loving heavenly Father who is on the other end of the ever-open line.

Now I am a father. And I would be very upset if someone told me that my children didn't think they could talk to me because they didn't know enough 'posh' words. And I would also be very sad if I heard that they felt there were some things they shouldn't talk about with me. I love them! They're my children!

A loving father wants to share in everything with his children. And there isn't a more loving dad (remember about the meaning of '*abba*'?) than God.

So *please*, *please* forget these false ideas, and feel you can talk to God simply and honestly about anything and everything.

DIFFERENT TYPES OF PRAYER

We talk in different ways when we are in different situations. There is the type of talking that is done when you stand up to address a large meeting. On a very different level is the type of talking and chatting that one does over the telephone.

Praying can take different forms also. Let me suggest four types of praying.

1. PRAYER IN CHURCH SERVICES

This is usually 'formal', which is another way of saying it has shape or form. If a large congregation is to be kept together in prayer we can't pray easily about little Freddy's bad toe. Mind you – if Freddy is really sick then the subject is big enough.

The point is that prayers in church have to be about things that concern everyone in the service. They have to be clear and easy to follow or people will get 'lost'. The

1. Matt. 6:6

prayers are usually spoken by one person on behalf of everyone else.

What the rest of us have to do is to follow carefully and when we say 'amen' at the end it's like adding our signature to a letter. 'Amen' means 'so be it'; and when we say the word we are agreeing with the prayer and making it our prayer also.

2. PRAYER IN A GROUP

The new Christian will sooner or later find himself or herself in a group where everyone is allowed to lead in prayer. Some people feel quite uneasy and even frightened by such groups. Some feel that if they don't take their turn in leading in a prayer they will be frowned upon.

Rubbish!

If you don't feel able to say a prayer out loud then don't worry about it. Just add your amen to the prayers of others and talk quietly in your heart to your heavenly Father.

However it's a pity if you never feel able to pray aloud with others so here's a few simple hints.

1. Remember nothing is different. It's still a matter of talking to your heavenly Father.
2. The only difference from private prayer is that you are surrounded by your brothers and sisters.
3. *Start by addressing the prayer.* Say something like: *Dear Heavenly Father.*
4. *Finish by signing off* – say: *for Jesus's sake, Amen.*
5. *Put your request simply in the middle!*

Suppose you want to pray for a little boy that everyone in the room knows has just had an accident. Here's how to do it simply:

Address:	Dear Heavenly Father
Request:	Please comfort and heal the little boy we heard about.
Sign off:	For Jesus's sake. Amen.

Simple isn't it! Remember group prayer meetings are rarely the place to pray for your own private needs. When you pray in a group you are leading the others in prayer. So don't say, 'Dear Heavenly Father *I* pray for . . .' but 'Dear Heavenly Father *we* pray for . . .'

The signing off words 'for Jesus's sake' are not some magic charm to make sure the prayer is answered. They are meant to remind us that all our prayers must be asking for the sort of things that Jesus would want.

(We could never pray: '*Dear Heavenly Father may my boss walk under a bus – for Jesus's sake!*').

Praying in a group is something that comes easier with practice but it is never a virtue to be able to go on and on. Keep your prayers clear, simple and short.

3. PERSONAL PRAYER TIMES

Every Christian should try to set aside at least one *fixed point* in the day for a personal prayer time. The obvious times are getting-up-time and just before going to bed. But there are no rules as to when.

In a way, a personal prayer time is a time of tuning-in to the ever-open line. It is valuable in itself but it also reminds us that we can chat to our Father at any time.

It is good to work out a pattern for the personal prayer time. Let me suggest (and it's only a suggestion) a pattern:

1. *Be quiet for a moment.* Try to shut out other thoughts and try to remember that God is with you and listening in. Thank him for being present.
2. *Look at something in the Bible.* We shall discuss this more in the next chapter. Many people find Bible-reading schemes like those of the Scripture Union a help. Others find help from books like *Living Light* or *Every Day* which give a selection of Bible passages to read for every day in the year.

3. *Talk over with God anything that occurs to you after reading the Bible.*
4. *Share with him the other things that are on your mind.*
5. *Remember before God anything else you feel you 'ought' to pray about.* I keep a little notebook to remind me of all sorts of things and people.
6. *Finish with a thankful moment of quietness.* Your Father has heard both the things you have said and the things you didn't get around to saying. He will be with you during the day. Praise the Lord!

Now this is just a suggestion. I suggest you try it for yourself for a few weeks and then see how you are getting on. Don't attempt too much too soon.

4. CONTINUOUS PRAYER

Paul told the Christians in Rome to 'pray at all times'. He said the same to the Christians in Thessalonica and added: 'be thankful in all circumstances'.

This is a call to make full use of the ever-open line. Keep sending up the messages. Keep thanking God quietly for all the good things (yes and the challenges that some of the not-so-good things sent us).

There's a story in the Old Testament about Nehemiah. He was a Jew who worked in the Court of the Emperor Artaxerxes of Persia. Nehemiah was deeply anxious to be allowed to go back to his homeland and do something about the broken-down City of Jerusalem.

Plucking up his courage, he told the Emperor about the desperate state of Jerusalem. And this is what we read:

The emperor asked, 'What is it that you want?' I prayed to the God of Heaven, and then I said to the emperor, 'If your Majesty is pleased with me ... let me go to the land of Judah ...'[2]

2. Neh. 2:4, 5

Notice the bit about praying. Nehemiah couldn't say, 'Excuse me, emperor, I must dash off and pray for a moment.' All he could do was send up a quick prayer on the ever-open line. Some people call this sort of prayer an 'arrow prayer'; shooting a thought or request up to heaven.

It doesn't matter what you call it. Do it! And keep on doing it. That's what the ever-open line is for.

PRAYING WHEN YOU DON'T KNOW IT

Sometimes people feel that their praying is at a low ebb or that they just cannot pray. When they tell me this I usually point to some words in the letter to the Romans:

> . . . the Spirit also comes to help us, weak as we are. For we do not know how we ought to pray; the Spirit himself pleads with God for us in groans that words cannot express.[3]

I think these are wonderful words! What Paul is saying is that the Holy Spirit who links us with our heavenly Father actually does our praying for us! He translates the deep feelings inside us into prayers that the Father will accept and answer.

Sometimes when someone says, 'I feel so low I just can't pray,' I say, 'Rubbish – you are praying all the time! The Spirit is doing it for you. Just fix your mind on the feeling inside and realise that your Father knows about it!'.

Many Christians find this is the only way to pray when they are overjoyed or over-worried, or when they just don't know what to pray for. They don't feel any words can express what's going on inside them. So they just remember the ever-open line; they hold up the feeling to God, trust that the Spirit is praying for them; and either don't speak at all, or simply move their lips quietly.

It can be a very profound way of praying for some. But

3. Rom. 8:26

if you don't find it helps you – don't let that bother you.
Your heavenly Father is still picking up the messages!

THE LORD'S PRAYER

Jesus gave his followers a pattern prayer. We usually
call it *The Lord's Prayer* or *The Family Prayer*. In these
days when there are so many new translations of the Bible
and modern services the Lord's prayer tends to be translated
in different ways. We shall look here at the version used in
the Series Three Church of England services.

What I want you to do is to notice the simple lessons it
teaches

Our Father in heaven   We address God in the way
only a Christian can. Because
of what Jesus has done for us,
and because we have put our
trust in Jesus, we are God's
children and he is our Father.

hallowed be your Name   Notice the capital 'N' for
name. In the Bible the *Name*
means everything about a
person. 'Hallowed be your
Name' is a way of saying
'everything about you is special'. So God is our Father –
but what a special Father he
is!

your kingdom come   Before we ask about what we
your will be done on   want, we remind ourselves that
earth as in heaven   what God wants is more important than anything else.
And we are telling God that
we ourselves want his will to
be done all around us.

107

Give us today our daily bread

Our Father is interested in our everyday needs. It is right to pray for ordinary things.

Forgive us our sins as we forgive those who sin against us

Jesus taught very clearly that if we don't forgive others we can hardly expect our Father to forgive us [Matt. 6:14, 15].

Do not bring us to the time of trial but deliver us from evil

If God is guiding us through life then it makes sense to ask him to keep us from testing and evil. The point of these words is that it makes us realise that we need all the help God can give us in daily life.

For the Kingdom, the power and the glory are yours now and for ever. Amen.

We end by reminding ourselves of the Father's greatness. We have been talking to the King of Kings and Lord of Lords. The last words of a time of prayer should be those of deep respect and adoration!

Questions
1. What are the wrong ideas that can make praying difficult?
2. What is the thing to remember about God that makes prayer easier?
3. What are the simple guidelines that make it easy to pray aloud in a group?
4. What is the value of a personal prayer time?

5. What does it mean to say: 'for Jesus's sake'?
6. What do you say to a Christian who is worried about feeling that he cannot pray?

Passages to Read
1. Matt. 6:5–15
2. Phil 4:6, 7
3. Col. 4:2–4

13: God's Reference Library

Wally Summers, the famous T.V. producer, leaned back in his chair and looked at his team of researchers. He knew he had the best available; intelligent and hard-working.

'O.K.,' he said, 'so we're agreed. In two week's time we meet here and you fellas bring me everything there is to know about this Jesus of Nazareth. And I do mean everything. We want this programme to put over the facts and we want our viewers to grasp what made him and his followers tick!'.

The researchers left the long conference table and went out to set about their task.

Two weeks later they were back. Frank Walters was first to speak.

'Well – we've dug up four accounts of the life of Jesus of Nazareth. I gather there are one or two fake versions in ancient literature but no one down the centuries takes them seriously.

'Of these four accounts, three seem to go about it the same sort of way but one has a very different feel about it. It seems to get inside the things that happened and suggest why. There's a lot of insight into the character and nature of Jesus.'

'The others?' questioned Wally.

'Well, they set out a basic picture about his birth and death and – er – this rising again business. They bring together things Jesus said, incidents with other people, what he taught his close followers, things he did like miracles and so on.'

'Do these accounts agree with each other much? Did you find lots of contradictions?' asked Wally.

'Very few,' said Frank. 'In fact just one or two little things that at first sight don't square with each other. But there was nothing of any importance, and I reckon a bit more thinking about it could probably get them sorted out.'

Wally grinned. 'They must have been looking over each other's homework!'.

'That's the surprising thing,' replied Frank. 'They can't have been. The experts we checked with assure us that they were written in different places at different times – they say that there probably was a certain amount of stuff they had in common; but not all that much.'

'Yes well,' ... said Wally getting a little uneasy. 'What else have we got?' It was Tom Scott who answered – pushing his glasses up his nose as he always did when he felt nervous.

'I've got this thing called the Acts of the Apostles.'

'So?'

'Well, it spells out what the close followers did after –er– after ...'

'After what?' snapped Wally.

'Well – after this business of Jesus sort of taking off – er – leaving the world. You know – what present-day Christians call the Ascension.'

'O.K. I understand – at least I don't, but I know what you mean. So what did you find?'

'Well, we have this piece of writing by a man called Luke who was a doctor probably from Philippi.'

'Go on'.

'Quite simply – it tells how the first believers in Jesus took the message throughout the Middle East and started churches all over the place. It's pretty exciting reading!'

'Lots of these miracles I suppose,' said Wally, with a look that showed he had 'heard it all before'.

'Well, quite a few,' said Tom. 'But as a journalist I must say I was pretty impressed. You know, those first Christians got into some bad scrapes and they didn't always come out of them alive. They weren't always converting everyone in sight. Indeed their star performer Paul of Tarsus got nowhere in some places. Another thing, their heroes aren't written up as perfect people. You can see the odd quarrel and bit of tension. You can feel the pressures they worked under.'

'Well,' said Wally with a sly smile. 'We seem to have a convert in our midst!' Tom Scott went slightly pink and pushed his glasses up his nose.

'Not exactly. But I'll tell you this. I've sifted through some pretty way-out old documents and stories for you in the past, but this isn't one of them. The man who wrote the Acts of the Apostles was a real man, and he genuinely believed in what he was saying. What's more the experts we talked with said that historical researchers have found Luke's details of the period amazingly accurate.'

'Yeah,' broke in Frank. 'This Doctor Luke character wrote one of the accounts of the life of Jesus that I was looking at. He seemed pretty keen to pin-point dates and things like that. I got the feeling he was writing well-researched stuff.'

'And the description of a shipwreck,' added Tom warming to the theme. 'Wow – if we could only film it as he writes it, it would be terrific!'

Wally began to feel uneasy. After all, he and his team were simply planning just another programme. 'O.K., O.K.,' he blustered. 'So it's got you all excited. That's fine. But don't forget we're just looking for facts. What else have we got?'

It was Bill Felton's turn. He also seemed to be quietly excited about the papers in front of him.

'I managed to find a pile of letters that those first Christians wrote to each other and to the various groups of believers they had got going.'

'Well done,' said Wally. 'So what have we got.'

'A lot of inside information into the lives those first Christians led. You know – the problems they faced; the pressures to conform to those around them.'

Wally leant forward, his chin resting on his hands. He could see that Bill was not finding it easy to express what he wanted to say. For once he didn't push.

'It's hard to – er – put it into words really,' continued Bill. 'I could spell out all sorts of ideas and teachings that run through these letters. But there's something more ... A sort of feeling that here were real people who had found something important and life-changing. And it had put them at odds with the Jews and at odds with the Roman authorities. And yet they didn't care. These men were full of joy and hope!'

Bill stopped short. 'Joy' and 'hope' were not exactly the sorts of words that researchers used when discussing 'just another T.V. programme'. There was an awkward silence and then Tom came in.

'I think I can see what Bill's getting at. There's a blazing sincerity about these people. They weren't fools. They knew the risks and they were ready to face them. But they weren't plaster saints either.'

'That's it!' Bill agreed. 'In fact some of the letters I looked through were written to sort out squabbles, personality-clashes and differences over their beliefs.'

Wally leaned back in his chair again with a grin. 'Looks like some of our modern Christians ought to get their noses into this stuff!' The researchers nodded vigorously.

113

Coffee was brought in and the business of passing round cups, sugar and biscuits eased the tension that had been building up. But not for long.

It was Colin Bartlett's turn to spell out some of the background to Jesus he had found. 'Jesus was a Hebrew,' he said. 'So I thought I ought to look into all the Hebrew writings that he talked about. You know their holy writings about God and the history of the Jews and them being a special people to God, and all that.'

'Good thinking,' agreed Wally, playing with his teaspoon.

'Yes,' Frank interrupted. 'All the time I was reading those accounts about Jesus, I got the feeling that I could get more of the meaning if I knew those background writings.'

Colin went on to give an account of the types of writings that made up the Hebrew Scriptures – as they are called. There were books that spelled out the opening of the link between the family of Abraham and the God who was so real to him that it was like talking to a friend.

There were lists of rules and codes that said how those who believed they were God's people should live. This God of Abraham was interested in a just and ordered way of life.

There was the remarkable history of the Hebrew people. They way they escaped through the Red Sea from Egypt. How they conquered the land of Canaan. How they tried to live with God as their only King but later gave it up and copied the types of government of other countries round about.

And there was the no-holds-barred history about how they ran their nation; about political upheavals; religious revivals; splits within, and onslaughts from the powerful nations round about.

Colin was obviously moved about the Hebrew religious poetry he had discovered. 'I found a lot of it getting right to where I am and showing my weaknesses and needs.

'And I found myself wanting to wave a flag for those people they called prophets,' he said.

'What – for fortune-tellers!' said Wally looking at Colin as if he was going cranky.

'No!' said Colin looking Wally straight in the eyes. 'That's what I thought. But the prophets were men who were sure that God had sent them to reform their country and to get people to be more faithful. They forecast what would happen if people didn't turn back to putting God first. In *that* sense they talked about the future.

'But in the main they were pitching in to the situation of their own day. Every now and again they came out with some uncanny insights about the future and about someone who was coming to their people and who would be really special . . .'

'That's right,' said Frank suddenly. 'You only have to read the accounts of Jesus to see that he is claiming – and others are claiming for him – that he's the special person the old writings talked about!

'Only he's not just for the Hebrews,' said Tom. 'He's for all of us!'

Wally felt a strange excitement creeping through him. He had never held a conference quite like this one. He could see that whatever those ancient documents were, they had got right into the very souls of his young researchers. The room was strangely silent.

Beside him, Sally, his secretary, had stopped taking notes and was glancing at him with a look that seemed to be saying, 'What do we do now?' Finally Wally spoke, quite quietly.

'So it looks like we've got a big programme on our hands!'

'I think we've got the biggest programme we'll ever do,' said Frank. The other two nodded. Wally found himself nodding.

'Say!' he said suddenly. 'Where did you fellas dig up all this fantastic stuff?'

The three researchers looked at each other and grinned. 'You tell him,' said Colin to Tom.

'Well, it was easy,' he said picking a black, leather-bound book out of his briefcase. 'It's all in the Bible!'

Wally's eyes widened. 'So that's what the Bible's all about,' he said. 'Hey, Sally. Go out and get me a Bible. It looks like I ought to do some researching for myself!'

* * *

And like Wally, our imaginary tough T.V. producer, we should all do some researching for ourselves!

WRONG IDEAS

People often have the wrong ideas of the Bible. They think it's some weird 'holy' book that's got nothing to do with life. Or they believe someone who says it's just a collection of 'myths' and full of contradictions.

I usually find that those who talk like that have never seriously read the Bible for themselves!

WRONG USES

Again, there are those who take the Bible quite seriously but use it in the wrong way. They pick out sentences (or 'verses' as we call them) from all over the place, bring them together and try to make them prove all sorts of strange views. The Jehovah's Witnesses do this, and so do many other groups who are usually trying to prove some pet idea.

And, quite frankly, many real Christians make the mistake of doing the same thing. Often they are trying to prove the right things – but they are going about it the wrong way.

NO MAGIC CHARMS

Whatever you do – don't use the Bible like a magic-charm book; sticking in a pin and seeing if God has a word for you by so doing. There's a famous old preacher's story about this. A man, wanting to know God's guidance opened the Bible and looked at the first thing that came to his eyes. It said:

'And Judas went and hanged himself.'

He jumped quickly to another place. It said:

'Go and do thou likewise.'

Not very helpful! No – we need to read the *books and chapters* of the Bible as books and chapters. And verses by themselves must only be used in the way they are used in the sections they come from.

WE ARE RESEARCHERS

Jesus is the most important person of all time. He is the one who actually *is* God's 'word' to men. If we want to find out as much as we can about him and know how he wants us to live for him, then we have to do what the T.V. researchers in our story did. We have got to dig into everything that was written about him by those who knew him. And that's what the Bible is all about.

NOT TOO DIFFICULT

We are very lucky in the twentieth century. There are very many helps available that make the Bible jump out of history and speak to us today.

And remember – that the 'speaking to us' *is a speaking of God's word*. We are not talking about some spare-time interest. We are talking about the main way God speaks to his children.

What are these helps? First of all, believe it or not, your local clergyman! He has been trained to understand the

Bible and to be able to teach from it. Obviously when we are dealing with what men wrote down centuries ago, there needs to be some specialist knowledge of the background and times. Men and women in the ministry of the churches have learned a great deal of that specialist knowledge.

Don't hesitate to ask them questions about the Bible. They would rather be asked those sorts of questions than any others.

BIBLE READING SCHEMES

Then there are organisations like the Scripture Union and Bible Reading Fellowship[1] who have specialised in working out personal Bible reading schemes for people of all ages and of all levels of education.

They not only suggest helpful ways of breaking the Bible up into short passages for everyday reading, they can also provide clearly written notes that pick up the knotty points and explain important background details which make the passage you are reading come alive.

And they are not afraid to point out the lessons to learn from those Bible readings for us today. The Bible is a living book.

In the last chapter we thought about the importance of a daily Personal Prayer Time. I mentioned the value of reading the Bible at such a time and very many of my Christian friends combine their daily Bible reading Scheme with their time of prayer. This is good. But I would give one word of warning.

Don't start tying yourself down to the wrong sorts of rules about Bible reading and prayer. Sometimes I meet people who feel they are sinning badly because they have fallen behind with their dated daily Bible readings. Of course they aren't! It would, of course, be better not to have

1. Scripture Union, 47 Marylebone Lane, London, W1.
Bible Reading Fellowship, 2 Elizabeth Street, London, SW1.

fallen behind but most of us do from time to time. I certainly do.

And when I do, I don't try to catch up the readings I've missed. I go straight to the reading for the day and start again. My advice is this. Set yourself as a goal to aim at – a daily prayer time linked to Bible reading. You will never regret such a good habit.

But if you miss the goal one day (or for several days running) don't think that God loves you any less. Just start going for the goal again.

BOOKS

Any Christian bookshop will amaze you with the vast number of helpful books to encourage an understanding of the Bible. I strongly recommend *The Lion Handbook to the Bible*. Ask for it next birthday – it's a wealth of information, colour photographs, maps, charts and so on.

And there are many more great books available. I strongly recommend buying modern translations of the Bible such as *The Good News Bible* and the *New International Version*.

NOT A BOOK TYPE

'But,' you say, 'I'm not the book-reading type.' Maybe that's true – but just be very sure you are not making excuses. You are, it seems, reading these words!

There are indeed many people who learn more from talking together about things than from reading about them on their own. And this is true with the Bible. That's why most churches these days encourage Bible study groups at all sorts of different levels. Ask your clergyman what your church has to offer.

BUT CAN WE TRUST THE BIBLE?

The Church of England Prayer Book calls the Bible 'God's Word written'. It's a pretty fantastic claim. How can we be so sure? There seem to be some pretty strong arguments about parts of the Bible being unscientific and so on.

The reason why I haven't tried to defend the Bible is that I want you first to discover it. Far too many objectors to the Bible speak from very little knowledge of it. Any intelligent Christian who wants to be honest must face up to the challenges about the Bible. But he needs first to have 'got into it' and begun to understand both what the Bible is and what it isn't.

In the years ahead you have a lot to learn and a lot to think out. But that is not a bad thing. In the meantime, God has given us all an exciting reference library. Let's start doing our own researching. What we will find will be more than 'interesting'. It will change our lives for the better!

Questions

1. What is the Bible?
2. Why should we all try to read the Bible?
3. In what way is the Bible God's word?
4. Why should we not jump around in our Bible reading?
5. Why is it good to link Bible reading to our prayers?
6. Who is the central person in the Bible?

Passages to Read

1. 2 Tim. 3:10–17
2. Luke 4:1–12 (Notice our Lord's trust in and obedience to what is written in the Scriptures.)

Appendix

THE TEN COMMANDMENTS – WHY THEY MATTER

The Commandments* are too lofty for the best of us and our loving God forgives our failings. But they are still very important. They remind us how much we need God's forgiveness and they set us goals to aim at in daily life.

1. I am the Lord your God: you shall have no other gods but me.

a) This looks very lofty and awe-inspiring (and so it is). But notice God speaks to his people and and says, 'I am ... *your* God'! What a wonderful thing! Our God is a person who takes a loving interest in people.

b) But if we are to know the full joy of God *belonging* to us then we must fully *belong* to him. There must be no rivals to God as our number one loyalty in life.

* The version of the Ten Commandments used here is that used in the Series Three Service of Holy Commission except where indicated.

2. You shall not make for yourself any idol.

a) The Israelites were surrounded by people who worshipped idols. They were under pressure to be like them (see Chapter Eleven).

b) But making idols here didn't mean going to other gods, it meant squeezing the real God into a shape (in every sense) that is too small, making the God Jesus talked about a sort of lucky charm. Do we have a picture of God that is too small and more comfortable to live with?

3. You shall not dishonour the name of the Lord your God.

a) Of course using God or Christ's name in swearing is a breaking of this Commandment. But it is not the main meaning.

b) Anything we do that is seen as having something to do with God but is not done in the just and loving way of God, is dishonouring to his 'name'. Just as a bad example of a Ford car dishonours the good name of that company. Quite a thought isn't it!

4. Remember the Lord's day and keep it holy.

a) The Christian observes Sunday as the Lord's day – the Jews observe Saturday. Christians made the switch to mark the fact that Jesus rose on the Sunday.

b) One purpose of the day is rest and a break from normal work. God says we need one day's rest in seven. We ignore this 'maker's instruction' at our peril!

c) And if we see this rest is important then we need to try to help others to rest and not to have to work on Sundays.

d) But the day is not just for our benefit – it is *for God*. It is our duty to worship him and to make a special point of putting his interests before our own.

5. Honour your father and your mother (so that you live a long time in the land I am giving you. *G.N.B.*)

a) The honouring of our parents is a way we honour God himself.

b) The words in brackets are the words that follow-on where the Series Three quotation leaves off. If we want peaceful countries and stable lives then we need to start with discipline in the family. It may not be a popular word but it's important (wait till *you* have children!)
We learn what government and law and order is all about in our home life. If we all learn badly, we shall make a mess of the government, law and order of bigger set ups – towns, and whole nations.

6. You shall not commit murder.

a) This Commandment is not broken if we kill someone accidentally or if we do so in a just war [Deut. 20] or if in the case of capital punishment [Gen. 9:6]. It is a terrifying awesome thing to take someone's life because God has himself given the gift of life.

b) Jesus went further. He said we had broken this Commandment in our minds and hearts if we hated or despised someone [Matt. 5:21, 22]. Everyone else is equally loved by God and we must always remember that.

7. You shall not commit adultery.

a) Adultery is 'having sex' with a person who is married to someone else. So it is stealing a husband or wife. A sexual act between two unmarried people is called *fornication* rather than adultery and this is also condemned in the Bible [Matt. 15:19].

b) Remember, this law sets out the 'lines on the field' and shows what is 'out of play'. But God wants his children to have fun and joy from the gift of sex in marriage. He is not a 'killjoy'.

c) Once again Jesus wanted us to see that we can commit adultery in our thoughts so there are battles to win there [Matt. 5:27–28].

8. You shall not steal.

a) This Commandment shows us that God is not against the idea of us *owning* things and having possessions (but see Chapter Eleven).

b) We need to remember that we can *steal time* as well as things. If we are paid to work eight hours and slip off early – that's stealing.

9. You shall not be a false witness.

a) This Commandment shows that God demands that we do not say what is not true about other people. This is the main meaning of the Commandment as originally given.

b) Of course there are plenty of places in the Bible which show that God wants the highest standards of honesty at all times.

10. You shall not covet anything that belongs to your neighbour.

a) Stealing and materialism begin with coveting, the burning feeling inside of wanting what others have.

b) The Bible speaks of coveting as a type of idol worship – it shows what we really put first in life [Eph. 5:5].